For my husband and my boys—becaus. 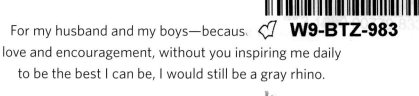 love and encouragement, without you inspiring me daily
to be the best I can be, I would still be a gray rhino.

"There's a reason parents flock to read the Orange Rhino—she helps us feel better about ourselves as parents when we blow it entirely—and who doesn't, sometimes? But *Yell Less, Love More* isn't just a feel-good book. It's a full-blown program to stop yelling, complete with day-by-day action steps, revelations, and original, powerful tips. As you follow this program, you'll be able to feel your brain rewiring. And in a few months, you'll look back and realize you can't remember the last time you yelled. Well-organized, motivational, funny, supportive, and EFFECTIVE!"

—Dr. Laura Markham, author of *Peaceful Parent, Happy Kids*
and founder of www.ahaparenting.com

"With wisdom and humor, Sheila quickly becomes an encouraging friend and mentor who gently teaches you how to manage your frustrations while building your self-confidence. You'll have fun reading this ultimate self-help book and will find yourself turning to it for love, support, and guidance when you fear you may be losing ground."

—Laura Deutsch, co-founder of Mommybites (mommybites.com)

"I loved every word of this book. Sheila's advice is honest, humorous, and most important, effective! As a clinical social worker and a mother of two young daughters, I highly recommend *Yell Less, Love More* both personally and professionally."

—Carla Naumburg, Ph.D., author of *Parenting in the Present Moment*

"*Yell Less, Love More* is a quick-witted and lighthearted read written by a mom who has been there and isn't afraid to bare all, from her fist-pumping wins to her most embarrassing lows. Sheila doesn't sugarcoat or finger-wag, she walks with you. I finished the book with an overwhelming feeling that I can do this; I can yell less and show my kids that love is what I have for them. This book is how we're all going to get there—sanity, humor, and heart all intact."

—Galit Breen, blogger, writer, mama of three, and converted yeller

"An absolute MUST-read for all parents. Sheila's friendly, honest voice is like a dear friend helping you through and cheering you on!"

—Melissa Kaye, co-founder of Mommy Business (mommybusiness.net)

"This book is a lifeline to regain hold of your sanity and help you stop yelling at your children. With Sheila's practical and doable ideas you can uncover the calm and caring parent you always hoped you'd be. She doesn't make you feel guilty; she empowers you and shows you how anyone can start from today and truly *Yell Less and Love More.*"

—Alissa Marquess, founder/editor of CreativeWithKids.com

First published in the USA in 2014 by
Fair Winds Press, a member of
Quarto Publishing Group USA Inc.
100 Cummings Center
Suite 406-L
Beverly, MA 01915-6101
www.fairwindspress.com
Visit www.bodymindbeautyhealth.com. It's your personal guide to a happy, healthy, and extraordinary life!

18 17 16 15 14   2 3 4 5

ISBN: 978-1-59233-633-3

Digital edition published in 2014
eISBN: 978-1-62788-177-7

Library of Congress Cataloging-in-Publication Data available

Cover and book design by Carol Holtz
Page layout by *tabula rasa* graphic design
Photography by Christine DeSavino

Printed and bound in Canada

The information in this book is for educational purposes only. It is not intended to replace the advice of a physician or medical practitioner. Always seek the advice of your physician or other qualified health care provider with any questions or concerns. Any reliance on any information provided here within is solely at the user's discretion and risk.

A 30-Day Guide That Includes

• 100 Alternatives to Yelling   • Simple, Daily Steps to Follow   • Honest Stories to Inspire

YELL LESS

L♥VE MORE

How The Orange Rhino® Mom Stopped Yelling at Her Kids—and How You Can Too!

Sheila McCraith

Creator of The Orange Rhino Challenge®

Fair Winds Press
100 Cummings Center, Suite 406L
Beverly, MA 01915

fairwindspress.com • quarryspoon.com

Gray Rhinos: Tenacious and vigorous animals who are naturally peaceful, but display aggressive behavior and charge when provoked.

Orange Rhinos: Determined and energetic people who choose not to charge with words, but to remain calm, loving, and warm when provoked or triggered.

CONTENTS

The Orange Rhino Story

I am a mom to four wonderful boys: James, Edward, Andrew, and Mac. I am not a professional in any field related to the topics covered in this book. The only Ph.D. I have is that I am a **P**arent (who) **H**as (the) **D**etermination to yell less and love more.

I am a recovering yeller.

I used to crawl into bed at night crying to my husband that I ruined yet another bedtime by yelling incessantly at my boys to "hurry up," "stop fighting," and "just get in bed, already!" I would try and shrug off the intense guilt and pain I felt from my horrific behavior so I could fall asleep, but I would inevitably just stay awake thinking about how awful I felt as a person, as a parent. I would stay awake thinking, *"How, oh how, did I ever get to this point where it feels like all I do is yell? How have I become this person? I never dreamed I'd be a yelling mom, and yet here I am. I wasn't yelled at. I rarely yell at anyone else. So why, oh why, am I yelling at my kids nonstop? I love them so much. What is wrong with me? No one else I know yells at their kids. What, oh what, is wrong with me?"*

I had this inner dialogue with myself for a good several nights a week for months. It was a horrendous dialogue to have so regularly, but I couldn't escape it. I could only hide it. I feared judgment, isolation, and embarrassment if I shared my struggles, so I kept them to my husband and myself. The result? I felt incredibly *alone*, like I was the only person who struggled with yelling. I felt incredibly *ashamed* because no one I knew talked about struggling with yelling. I felt incredibly *nervous* because I had no idea how to stop my struggle with yelling.

As time passed, the gut-wrenching guilt in my stomach started lasting longer than a few hours at night and my boys' tears and responses started tearing into my heart deeper and deeper. I knew that yelling hurts my kids, that it scares my kids, that it shames my kids, and that it does anything but show my love for my kids. And even though I knew that I wanted to change, I couldn't find the resolve, the courage, or the determination to fully seek change.

Until January 20, 2012, that is—the day that ultimately led to the beginning of a new relationship with my boys, my husband, my life, and myself.

The Birth of The Orange Rhino Challenge

That Friday morning, our handyman caught me screaming at my boys, then ages five and under. We're talking red-in-the-face, body-shaking, full-on screaming! *I was mortified by my behavior … and then, after some soul searching, inspired to finally change my behavior.* I could no longer accept that yelling at my kids wasn't a problem. I could no longer accept all the excuses I had made as to why I couldn't change: I'm too tired, I don't have time, nothing else will work, the kids will grow and it won't be a problem. And I could no longer accept that my kids were starting to think of me as a screaming, mean, and scary mother instead of as the loving, patient, and firm, but kind, mother I always wanted to be, and deep down inside knew I could be.

I was done yelling. **The next morning, I committed to my family that I would go 365 days straight without yelling; that's right—straight!** If I yelled, I promised to reset my counter back to zero days. And if I really, really yelled, then I promised to set my counter back to negative two days. It was an intense goal with intense rules, but it fit my cold-turkey personality and was exactly what I needed to be motivated to turn my behavior around. I then launched a blog to publicly chronicle my progress and keep me accountable. But perhaps, even more so, I launched it in hopes of finding support and others struggling like me. Not only did I know I needed the help, but also, I no longer wanted to feel alone. (As it turned out, the more I publicly wrote about my struggles with yelling, the more I discovered moms, dads, grandparents, teachers, and caretakers from all over the globe who identified with my struggle and who understood my feelings of shame, disappointment, and frustration. I totally wasn't alone—and neither are you!)

At first I just called my blog the "No Yelling for 365 Days Project." But I yearned for something more; I yearned for an inspiring symbol for my challenge that I could look at in times of difficulty and be reminded of my promise. I struggled and struggled until one morning when I had corralled all the boys into the minivan. As I buckled James in, he screamed in my face. I calmly said to him, "James, if Mommy can't yell, what does that mean for you?"

He looked straight at me, finger in his nose, and equally calmly replied, "I can't yell, but I can still pick my nose!"

Ha! I couldn't help but laugh. That night, I Googled "origin of nose" and somehow ended up at "rhinoceros." Further "Googling" showed that rhinos are naturally calm and peaceful animals but that when provoked, display aggressive behavior and charge. Aha! I was totally a rhino; I can be a calm mom, but when provoked, I charge with my words! But oh, oh, how I no longer wanted to be a normal gray rhino; I no longer wanted to be aggressive. I no longer wanted to charge with my words. I wanted to be warm and loving like the color orange, and I knew I needed the determination and energy that orange symbolizes. So *voilà,* The Orange Rhino Challenge was born!

The Orange Rhino Challenge "Yelling Meter" and Challenge Details

It was great to finally have an inspiring name and symbol, but I had a bigger problem. I quickly realized that it was hard to define what "no yelling" actually meant! Could I raise my voice? What is a firm voice? What if I accidentally snap? What about in emergencies, can I yell then? So voilà, my "Yelling meter," was born and I strictly followed it until February 6, 2013, when I celebrated one year of not yelling!

The Orange Rhino Yelling Meter	
Acceptable	• **Level 0: The Everyday Voice.** The "life is good, I just love being a mom and having these little conversations" voice. Serenity and happiness ooze out with every word. Signs: You think to yourself, *"Wow, this is a nice moment, I think I'll cherish it,"* and you're filled with hope that the day is gonna be a good one.
	• **Level 1: The Whisper.** The quiet, almost inaudible voice that our preschool teacher uses that somehow gets attention, respect, and follow-through. Signs: You can barely hear it, and it works like magic.
	• **Level 2: The Re-direct Voice.** It's a clear, loving, and patient voice that does not show irritation for the situation at hand, but instead gently expresses that you don't like a behavior and why, and offers a new activity. Signs: When you use it, you pat yourself on the back for successfully following advice from a parenting magazine, for once.
	• **Level 3: The Firm Voice (potentially raised).** This is the "I am starting to mean business" voice accompanied by occasional raised eyebrows and introduction of idle threats. Signs: You are still calm and there are no hurt feelings, but you're wondering when (not if) you're gonna snap and you are growing impatient, quickly.

The Orange Rhino Yelling Meter	
Acceptable	• **Level 4: The "Oopsie" Snap.** "Stop! All right! Ouch!" This snap is starting to get nasty, but hasn't gotten there yet. It isn't a long tirade; it's just a quick, sharp, voice where you stop yourself ... it's just enough to make the kids stop what they are doing for a second and think whether or not they will continue annoying behavior. Signs: Blood pressure is picking up a little, but you are back to calm quickly and think, *"Oh shoot, I really didn't mean to do that."*
Not Cool, Back to Day 0	• **Level 5: The Nasty Snap.** "Darnit! Knock it off! Cut it out!" This snap might be short, but it's filled with venom. Signs: Blood is starting to boil inside; vocal chords are warming up, preparing for a long tirade; you think to yourself, *"Oh shoot, was that a nasty snap?"* If you think it, it was.
	• **Level 6: The Yell.** It's loud. You know it's loud. And it's mean. You simply know you've crossed the line, there is no question. Signs: Kids' tears are a pretty good indicator, as are doors slamming and kids screaming back at you that you're mean and they don't love you anymore.
So Not Cool, Back to –2 Days	• **Level 7: The Raging Scream.** A notch up from "the yell," it's totally intentional and is filled with much more nastiness, hurtfulness, and hysteria—on both sides. Signs: Body shaking, often hard to stop doing it; results in feelings of massive guilt and shame in the screamer (at least for me) and definite feelings of shame, sadness, and fear in the kiddos; throat throbs afterward.

IN CASE OF AN EMERGENCY (kid running off in parking lot, kid running into street, hot stove, etc.), I can use up to a level 6 voice but it has to be yelling *to* the kid not *at* the kid. When I yell *at* someone, it's mean. When I yell *to* someone, it's to get their attention. Said voice MUST be followed by firm voice in level 3 or below, otherwise it's no good.

How to Use This Book to Become an Orange Rhino

I am guessing that my "Yelling Meter" Challenge Details and year-long goal might have freaked you out a bit; I know they sure as heck did for me! *"What was I getting myself into?"* I thought. *"How was I going to actually go a year without yelling?"* I worried. Yep, I know from experience that the idea of learning to "Yell Less and Love More" is absolutely daunting and rightfully so! My journey was more than hard at times and I definitely experienced some "I'm so going to quit" moments. But, it was also a lot of fun and positively life changing. I can say with complete confidence that I am now not only a quieter person since I began The Orange Rhino Challenge, but I am also a happier, kinder, calmer, and stronger person. And, I can say with complete confidence that I wouldn't have made it to this better place without the phenomenally supportive Orange Rhino Community and the simple steps that I unintentionally took during my challenge. This book not only outlines these steps, but also breaks them down into even smaller steps so that the challenge of learning to yell less feels less daunting and more doable.

Knowing how stressful and exhausting parenting can be on a good day, and how some days offer little free time, I organized this book into thirty short, approachable, and easy-to-follow daily sections. Each day starts with a personal story followed by a summary of key revelations that kept me on track, suggested actions that reflect what I did on my journey, a favorite inspirational quote, and three daily tips to help you.

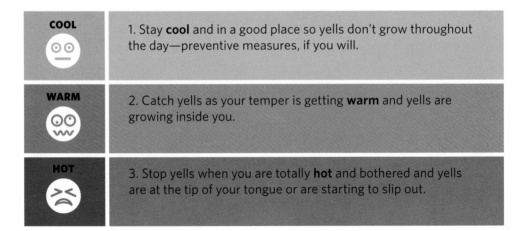

COOL	1. Stay **cool** and in a good place so yells don't grow throughout the day—preventive measures, if you will.
WARM	2. Catch yells as your temper is getting **warm** and yells are growing inside you.
HOT	3. Stop yells when you are totally **hot** and bothered and yells are at the tip of your tongue or are starting to slip out.

The only suggestion I have for you as you read through and use this book is that you remember **the first step to yelling less is to embrace that no "shoulds" are allowed when reading!** I am kind of joking, but mostly not! One of my biggest triggers for yelling is thinking about everything that I "should" be doing in parenting based on parenting books, articles, or discussions I have overheard. So, let this book guide you and give you ideas for your own journey to becoming an Orange Rhino, or let it tell you exactly how to set up your journey. There is no right way to use this book, except well, your way!

Do my Yelling Meter and Challenge Details create the framework you crave? Follow them! Do they not jive with you? Adjust them! Perhaps instead of setting back to day zero if you yell, stop the counter on the day the yell occurred and restart after a successful day.

Do you like to read books in one fellow swoop? Go for it! Or, read the book one day at a time, as designed. Miss a day? Have no fear. Yes, this is a thirty-day guide but if it takes you longer, that is cool, too.

Do you have just a little time each day? Perhaps read just the tips and revelations, which are clearly marked by colorful boxes for easy finding on those days when you have one full minute of peace!

Do you find my tips (e.g., yelling into the toilet and banging pots and pans to create a musical party to let off some steam) too crazy and silly? Then try the more traditional tips I share such as walking away, taking deep breaths, and taking preventative measures such as getting enough sleep.

Do you not have any time to read but want a great visual reminder to Yell Less and Love More? Well, then perhaps leave this book, with the cover visible, in high-yelling zones. Maybe it is a coaster in the kitchen? Or the first thing you see in the bathroom each morning? Again, I am kind of joking, but mostly not!

All kidding aside, the point is this: While this book is about my journey, it really is about your journey, too. So please remember not to worry or beat yourself up about what you "should" be doing while reading this book! You know what works best for you; trust yourself and your instincts.

Oh, and please, please, pretty please also remember that even if you are on your path to being an Orange Rhino, you are still human! **This journey isn't about perfection; it's about progress.** You might progress at the pace you wish, or you might not. Either way, it doesn't matter. What really matters is that you are progressing forward, that you are yelling less, and loving more, one moment at a time.

All my best to you on your journey,
The Orange Rhino,
a. k. a.

Sheila

1

Ease into Change

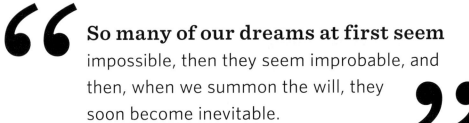

So many of our dreams at first seem impossible, then they seem improbable, and then, when we summon the will, they soon become inevitable.

—Christopher Reeve

I never dreamed that I would be a yelling parent. I also never dreamed that, after years of yelling, I would be able to become a nonyelling parent. Me, become a nonyeller? Impossible! I don't know how to get my kids' attention without yelling. I don't know how to manage my frustration over their constant fighting without yelling. I don't know how to handle my personal stress without yelling. Getting caught by the handyman yelling at my boys, however, gave me a strong will to make the impossible possible. Getting support from family, friends, strangers, and random orange objects such as sticky notes and orange napkins also kept that will strong and growing, even when I struggled in the beginning to get past one week of not yelling. Yes, it took me several tries to be able to toss all the yelling aside completely, but looking back, I realize I finally stopped after I had established some important basics. These first five days focus on those basics and create the groundwork that will help you make your dream of becoming a nonyeller not only possible, but inevitable.

Day 1

Admit the Need to Change:
Embracing My "Uh-Oh-I-Need-to-Change" Moment

Friday, January 20, 2012—The day that started out mortifying and ended up being inspiring; the day that I will never forget; the day that has truly come to symbolize the beginning of a new life for me.

James was five, Edward three and a half, Andrew two, and Mac just six months. I was thirty-four and yelled a heck of a lot more than I cared to share with anyone at that point in my life. As soon as I got Mac to sleep for his morning nap, I quietly rounded the older boys up and brought them into my room so that I could use the breast pump. I locked the door so that the boys couldn't sneak out and then attached myself to the machine, hopeful that my task would be completed before I needed to break up any fights that developed from being trapped in a room for ten minutes.

Exhausted from a "wonderful" night's sleep (not one, not two, but three of my boys had problems sleeping), my tolerance for shenanigans was at an all-time low. Well, not thirty seconds into pumping the boys found the spare pump parts—the back-up tubes, the piston for the hospital pump, the extra horns. Before I knew it my room had turned into a battle-field. While screaming (obviously, why be quiet during naptime?!), one son whipped the tubes like nunchucks, one used the piston as a sword, and the other catapulted the horns across the room. Then the boys intensified their game and started running around yelling even louder and jumping on and off my bed—you know, the bed that I had just made that was now *unmade*. Awesome.

I totally wanted to lose it. I wanted to stop the insanity. I just wanted some peace and quiet for ten minutes! Was that asking too much? Okay, I know, rhetorical question.

I nicely asked my boys to stop; to sit "crisscross applesauce" and tell me about what they would like to do that day. I tried reading them a book. Shoot, I tried every trick in the book so that I didn't become the raging lunatic that I can be when I'm pushed to the edge. Of course, nothing worked and as I was attached to the blessed boob-pump, I couldn't easily get up and intervene. Nope, I couldn't just walk ever so politely over to them, bend down and make eye contact, gently place my hand on their shoulders, and explain to them in preschool terms that if they didn't stop NOW mommy was going to friggin' lose it. You know, because that is what all the parenting books recommend—not the "lose it" part, of course, but the other parts. I politely asked them again to stop, and again, they ignored me (shocker).

So I did what I could do.

I did what I knew how to do.

I did what I had naturally started doing when I was frustrated with my kids.

I yelled.

Yes, the volcano that was me erupted. In a high-pitched and as-loud-as-I-can-go scream, I bellowed out, "STOP IT NOW. MOMMY JUST NEEDS A MINUTE OF PEACE TO REGAIN HER COMPOSURE. PLEASE. JUST. GIVE. ME. A. STINKIN'. MINUTE!" Finally, the silence I sought came, only to be interrupted by an unusual noise outside my bedroom door.

"Oh sh*t," I thought, "*someone is robbing the house.*" I nervously called out, "Hello?" More silence (and this time, I didn't seek it). I wanted to hear my husband's voice or the babysitter's. Finally, I heard some footsteps come down from the attic. "*What the…?*" I thought. I ushered the boys into the corner, ordered them to stay quiet, and ever so cautiously opened the door.

There stood Luke, our handyman. We had just finished nine months of house construction to make room for Mac and had come to trust all the workers to come and go as needed, so they had the garage code. It would have been really handy to have remembered that at the moment!

"Oh, hey Sheila, I'm just here fixing some things."

Chagrined, I responded, "Um, hi Luke, did you hear all that?"

With a big sh*t-eating grin on his face he replied, "Why, yes, yes I did. You go, mom. A mom's gotta do what a mom's gotta do."

I was MORTIFIED. MOR.TI.FIED!

Mortified that someone had caught me yelling.

Mortified that I hadn't caught myself before I started yelling.

Mortified that my struggles with yelling had grown to this new level.

I apologized to Luke for my outburst and turned to my boys and said, "I am so sorry. I love you very much. Mommy made a mistake and that was not the way to handle frustration." I stumbled through the rest of the day in a haze. While I was literally present with my boys, my mind, however, was not. It was going back and forth between thinking about how embarrassed and disappointed I felt and wondering how I had let things get to this point. In the midst of all my mental back and forth, I had a huge epiphany that changed my life.

> My boys are my audience—my most important, always-there audience; they are the ones who matter. They are the ones I love fiercely, the ones who watch me every day, learn from me every day, and hope for my affection every day!

I realized that in the nine months the workers basically lived with us, even though I was pregnant and extra hormonal, extra tired, and extra stressed, I still only yelled horrifically a handful of times because I felt like I had an audience, an audience that I wanted to impress. I had put every ounce of energy and self-control I had into ensuring I didn't yell because I wanted to *appear* like a great, loving, calm, and patient mom. And I succeeded. Why? Simply stated, because I feared judgment; I feared leaving the workers with a bad impression of me. My epiphany then exploded—I also realized that on the flip side, when I *am* alone, when I am without an audience, when I am without potential judgment from a coworker, a neighbor, or a friend, I put way less energy into finding the self-control to remain calm and I yell freely and more frequently at my boys, which is so backwards!

My boys *are* my audience—my most important, always-there audience; they are the ones who matter. They are the ones I love fiercely, the ones who watch me every day, learn from me every day, and hope for my affection every day! I didn't just want to *appear* loving and patient and yell-free in front of them; I wanted to be loving and patient and yell-free for them. My boys deserved for me to work just as hard to keep it together as I did at the grocery store, the coffee store, the park, or anywhere outside of the house. **What my boys thought of me was infinitely more important than what strangers would think of me. Period.** I didn't want my kids to think of me as a screaming, raging, mean, and scary mother. I wanted them to think of me as loving, patient, and firm, but kind. I wanted them

> I realized that my so-called disaster wasn't actually a disaster but an opportunity, an opportunity to admit to myself that I needed to change; an opportunity to admit to myself that I would no longer accept that my yelling was okay.

to judge me and proclaim, "My mommy is the bestest mommy ever!" I didn't want them to think that I was a "mean witch" or that "when you yell at me, it makes me think you don't love me anymore" (as I had been told).

My epiphany didn't stop there; it kept going, just like my yells used to, but in this case, the continuation was a good thing! At that moment I kind of felt like I was in the movie *Apollo 13* where the NASA director says to Gene Kranz, "This could be the worst disaster NASA's ever faced." And Gene replies, *"With all due respect, sir, I believe this is gonna be our finest hour."*

At first, when I got busted for yelling by our handyman, I felt like it was one of my worst personal disasters ever. EVER. But then, like Gene, I realized that my so-called disaster wasn't actually a disaster but an opportunity; an opportunity to admit to myself that I needed to change; an opportunity to admit to myself that I would no longer accept that my yelling was okay; an opportunity to push myself harder than ever to change, stop yelling, and have more finest hours with my boys.

And I was ready to change. I needed to change.

That mortifying, wickedly embarrassing moment had to be, and would be, the last of its kind. Sure, it was mild in the sense that my kids didn't hide in the corner and cry, or run away from me in tears, or stare at me in total fear, but that was luck and not the norm. Besides, while their responses were mild, my yelling was not. It was hot, hot, hot, and full of intention to scare and hurt my kids' feelings. Why? Why would I want to do that? I love my kids and certainly didn't want to be scary to them. I don't want to scare them!

Yes, the yelling had to stop. Yes, I had to change.

And I knew that I could change.

I mean, clearly I knew how to keep it together and not yell, because I did it for basically nine months at home, and I do it daily out in public. Knowing this, and having the epiphany that my kids are my most important audience, inspired me to start living a yell-free life not just outside the home, but inside too. Getting caught screaming at my children by someone I respect could have gone down as one of the worst moments in my life. Instead, it ended up being one of the best.

There are many yells in my life that I would take back—the one that morning, however, well, I wouldn't take it back. Nope. That is the one yell that I am eternally grateful for because it pushed me to start my journey to yell less and that has truly improved my entire family's life for the better.

Orange Rhino Revelations

- I didn't yell at my kids in front of others because I feared what "my audience" would think.

- The truth, though, is that my kids are my most important audience. I care more what they think about me than anyone else. I want them to think I am a loving, warm, and not scary person.

- If I can hold it together and not yell in public, I can do the same at home.

Today's Actions

- **Admit the need to change.**

- **Write down one of the most "disastrous" yelling moments you've had.** Be descriptive. How did you feel in the moment? Days or months later? What did your kids' faces look like? What did they say? How do you feel now writing it down?

_____

_____

_____

_____

- **Embrace your "disaster" moment.** Tell yourself it is no longer your worst moment ever but the best moment ever because in remembering it now, it is forcing you to admit that you need to change and inspiring you to change. Say out loud, "I need to change. This yelling has to stop." I know thinking about your "worst turned best" moment is not entirely comfortable. That said, though, when I find myself struggling to stay cool, I remember my handyman story and the embarrassment and sadness I felt. Doing so helps me stay inspired by reminding me why my journey started in the first place and why all the hard work most definitely needs to continue. So go ahead, push yourself to capture all the ugly feelings of that one moment (or a combination of several) so that you can let that moment no longer bring you down but help keep you up!

> **❝ It is during our darkest moments** that we must focus to see the light. **❞**
>
> —Aristotle Onassis

Today's Tips

COOL	**Orange Rhino Favorite:** Post pictures of your children as newborns in problem areas to remind yourself how fragile kids are and to proceed with gentle words.
WARM	Pretend there is a hidden camera in the TV; let the fear of judgment work wonders.
HOT	Sing your emotions. My favorite? "I want to yell-la-la-la-laaaaaa." Singing is unexpected, which gets my kids' attention and also helps me to relax.

The preciousness of a photo of my son as a newborn forces me to stop, slow down, and smile when I am in a huff—totally warms my heart and pushes the yell down.

Day 2

Ask Others for Support:
Help, It Does a Body Good

I admit it. I am the one in the house who taught my kids to swear. Of course, it was totally unintentional. I didn't just wake up and say to myself, *"Okay, today after I teach my son to say 'please' I am going to teach him to say 's**t.'"* It's just that before kids I had a wicked bad sailor's mouth, or potty mouth, or however you want to describe a mouth that swears readily as a form of communicating great displeasure or frustration. I knew that I did not want to raise my children using such words, so as soon as I had my first son, I started working really hard to curtail my swearing. Even so, sometimes a swear would slip out—and not in a whisper or mumble, as I intended.

As a result, I have unintentionally taught my boys a few four-letter words that really didn't need to be in their vocabularies. Yeah, not so proud. But I am proud of one four-letter word that I have *intentionally* taught each of my boys since they first starting making sounds: help.

Help: a four-letter word that I tell my sons they can't live without knowing.
Help: a four-letter word that I encourage my sons to use daily, whenever they are struggling.
Help: a four-letter word that I teach my sons by example by helping others.
Help: a four-letter word that I seemingly don't understand, embrace, or use for myself.

That's right. Every day when one of my sons gets frustrated with an art project, angry at a puzzle, mad at himself for not being able to achieve a task, or upset that he doesn't know the answers to schoolwork, I look him right in the eye and say, "Hey, it is okay to ask for help. Never be afraid or embarrassed to ask for help, okay?"

And I mean it. I really, truly mean it. And yet, I am the last person to ask for help for myself. I think I might even be allergic to asking for help! Really. Shortly after my fourth son was born, I was sitting at the preschool back-to-school meeting and someone asked what she could do to help me, seeing as I now had four boys under five and Mac was just one month old! Before I could speak, my two friends in the room replied in complete unison, "Don't bother asking. She won't accept help."

They were right. I wouldn't have accepted help, because I don't like to. I don't like asking for help and I don't like receiving it. I am not entirely sure why; it's silly, really. I have no problem helping others and never think twice about doing so; I love helping others. I just don't love being helped. For some reason it makes me feel embarrassed, nervous, and weak. I worry that I will be judged as a "not good enough mom" if I can't do it all on my own when so many others seem to be doing it so gracefully. I worry that people will think, *"Why did she have so many kids if she can't do it on her own?"* or *"Why does she accept help when she is too busy to give back as much? That's so selfish of her."*

> **I couldn't do it all, but what I could do was swallow my pride and realize that asking for help wasn't a sign of weakness, but a sign of strength.**

And perhaps most importantly, I worry that I will be disappointed with myself if I ask for help. For some ridiculous reason, I feel that I have to prove to myself and to the world that I can raise four boys without help.

Well, guess what? I can't. I can't do it all. I couldn't do it all, but what I could do was swallow my pride and realize that asking for help wasn't a sign of weakness, but a sign of strength. It was a sign of knowing what I needed in terms of support to make my sons' lives a little calmer, a little richer, a little better. When I had my third son, Andrew, I quickly realized that, with my husband gone Monday through Friday and my extended family four hours away, I not only needed help, but also I needed to actually accept help! I did my best; I got a babysitter for a few hours and I said "yes" more often when friends offered to do a pick-up or drop-off for me when I had to be in two places at once or had had the stomach bug. And yes, it was still very difficult to accept the help, even when I couldn't keep a saltine cracker down and desperately needed that help. Oh, I was so stubborn!

Clearly, by the time my fourth son came around, I hadn't made much progress in the asking for or accepting help department; in fact, I had regressed. I still stubbornly tried to do everything by myself; I used the babysitters sparingly, and I only said "yes" to help in emergencies. My friends would say it pained them to see me struggle so much when a simple "Will you please help me?" would have been so readily accepted.

I knew my thinking was backwards. How could I expect to truly teach my children to learn that it is okay to ask for help when I never modeled it for them? Yes, I was teaching them to be self-sufficient and to do things on their own, which are essential and important skills, but I also wanted to show them that asking for help is a necessary skill. Why? Because there are some things that you just can't do on your own—or maybe you could, but it would be that much harder. And why make something that is hard, harder?

Such as, for instance, learning to yell less.

I not only knew I would need help and support learning to yell less, but also I experienced no fear or embarrassment asking for it. I guess the enormity of The Orange Rhino Challenge, the fact that it seemed so unreachable and so difficult, made me intuitively know that I couldn't do it alone.

The minute I decided I was going to embark on The Orange Rhino Challenge, I emailed my husband, my mom, and two local friends and said something like, "Hey, I am going to try and go a year without yelling. But I will need your help every step of the way to keep me on track. Will you help me, please? Will you text me to tell me not to yell? Will you call and ask me how I am doing? Will you write and remind me of my promise? Will you let me yell at you instead? Kidding … kind of."

Guess what? They all said, "Yes of course we will help you," without hesitation and without judgment. Okay, I did get a few "You are nuts," but then they quickly added, "but that is awesome, good for you!"

I then told my Facebook world and, well, any acquaintance I knew, really! Yeah, I kind of made a big push to get help so that I would have a big group of people to be accountable to. Who would have thunk it?! Where was the stubborn "I don't do help" person I knew? **I had just started The Orange Rhino Challenge and it was already changing me!**

Asking for help was one of the greatest steps I have taken on this journey, and I have since discovered that when I ask for help during tough times, people from near and far tell me to keep going, to not give up, and to just keep pushing forward. Having support is such a huge part of this challenge. There are more texts out in the cyber world than I can count that read, "Help! I am going to lose my sh*t if they hit each other one more time" and "It's only 6:50 a.m. and I have wanted to yell at least five times. ARGHHHH!" And, there are equally as many texts from my support network that read, "Hang in there," "Don't quit!" and "You can do it!" Being able to gain strength and support from others has not only helped me curb a growing yell but also relieved me of stress.

I am certain that carrying the load of learning to yell less by oneself is doable. But I am also certain—no, I know for a fact—that I couldn't have learned to yell less as quickly and as painlessly without the help of others who believed in me and cheered me on.

Orange Rhino Revelations

- Asking for help is not a bad thing; it's a good thing. Asking for help doesn't make me weak; it makes me strong.

- Telling my story to others gave me strength by helping me see that I wasn't the only one struggling.

Today's Actions

- **Create a personalized support network.** Ask at least one person to fill each of the following roles. *Note: These people do not have to be nonyellers, they just need to believe in you and be supportive of you and your commitment. As Oprah Winfrey said, "Surround yourself only with people who are going to lift you higher." Do not for a minute believe anyone who says that you cannot learn to yell less, because you can learn to yell less and you will!*

  1. The Pep Talker: The person(s) you can call when you want to quit who will always tell you not to, that you can do it, and to remember why you started The Orange Rhino Challenge in the first place. Potential pep talkers: spouse, best friend, parent, or anyone you trust.

  2. The Texter/Tweeter: The person(s) attached to their phone who can be reached out to whenever you have the urge to yell. Choose someone preferably in the same time zone with roughly the same parenting schedule, someone who you know will be free to reply as soon as possible with a supportive "You can do it!"

  3. The Children: No explanation needed—I think you know who these people are! And yes, I told my kiddos my plan and write about it in Day 3.

- **Tell your support network your "worst-turned-best" story.** The more often you tell your "worst-turned-best" story and how you decided to change, the more it will motivate you to work hard to change and the more people you will get supporting you! Uncomfortable? Yes. Worthwhile? Absolutely.

If you are like me, you might have read the actions above and thought, *"Wait, having support means telling people that I need support, which means making my 'I yell too much' problem a slightly more public reality, which I so don't want to do."* I get that. It might not be too easy to ask for support, but again, trust me: You will need the support and telling people is necessary. Sharing my challenge made me more accountable, especially because anytime I spoke or saw someone from my support network, he/she would ask how my challenge was going, keeping me focused on my goal.

66 You can make it, but it's easier if
you don't have to do it alone. 99

—Betty Ford

Today's Tips

COOL	Set up your phone to remind you every thirty minutes not to yell; this might be annoying, but it's helpful!
WARM	Do push-ups instead of yelling a putdown! Exercise releases endorphins (or something like that), which calms you down. Added benefit? Much better-looking arms!
HOT	Say "I love you" over and over again; it is hard to yell when you realize how much you love someone.

Do a push-up so you don't have to yell a put-down.

Day 3

Get Your Kids to Help:
The Orange Rhino Game

I am often asked, "So, how many tries did it take you to go 365 days without yelling? How many times did you actually have to restart?" I "believe" the answer is ten, depending on how I count. Thanks to the adrenaline from having a successful first day, the support from others, and the determination to prove to people that I could do this, I made it eight consecutive days on my first official try at The Orange Rhino Challenge. And then it took me eight more tries before I made it an entire day again. It was completely like the movie *Groundhog Day* ... and completely and utterly frustrating.

I'd wake up and tell myself I can do this. Then I would get frustrated that I had yelled the day before, get all worked up and irritated over the smallest thing, and then BAM— I would yell. Then I'd go to sleep disappointed, and then wake up and tell myself I can do this. Then I would get frustrated that I had yelled the day before, get all worked up and irritated over the smallest thing, and then BAM—I would yell. Then ... well, you get the point. For eight straight days! It was miserable. Absolutely miserable. On Day 1, Take 6, I wrote on my blog:

> "So, James, how am I doing with not yelling?"
>
> "Terrible. Absolutely terrible. You just yelled at me the other day. And the other minute."
>
> Yeah, that was pretty much an accurate summary. I have no idea what has transpired since last week. Last week I went a whole eight days. And I felt so good. So so good. To all you nonyellers out there, I know you are laughing thinking to yourself, eight days is nothing. That is so easy. But to me, it was difficult. At first. That first day was EXHAUSTING. I remember coming up to bed after the day was over and saying to my husband, "Wow, I feel great from not yelling but darn am I tired."
>
> It took every bone in my body to keep it together. To find my inner preschool teacher voice that speaks quietly and lovely and still gets respect and response. But somehow I did it. ALL WEEK LONG I did it. Every day I went without yelling I felt more invigorated and it got easier. And it felt so utterly amazing. I felt an energy I haven't felt in years. I was bouncing off the walls with adrenaline and excitement.
>
> And yet, as my five-year-old pointed out just now, I am sucking at the whole not yelling thing right now.

Even though that week of not being able to get back on track was almost three years ago, I still remember how it felt as if it were yesterday. Oh, oh, I felt so demoralized and hopeless! I just couldn't get it together! I was yelling way more than I did before I even started The Orange Rhino Challenge ... and it was all self-inflicted. I put so much pressure on myself to succeed that I was crumbling at every hard moment. I felt so discouraged that I couldn't now go a day, or even half a day, that I tried less and less. I felt so embarrassed with my struggle that I thought I should just quit and save face.

Then miraculously, out of nowhere, when I was so ready to quit, a new idea came to me that turned out to not only be one of my best ideas ever, but also my saving grace during the entire challenge. This miraculous moment occurred Day 1, Take 6. Right after my son told me how much I was yelling, I looked at my boys and said, **"I need help. I need you to say, 'Orange Rhino' every time you can see that I am getting cranky, on edge, or really close to yelling.** Let's try. I am going to yell at you, but it's pretend, okay. It doesn't count!"

"OH MY GOSH I can't believe you spilled milk again!"

> I was yelling way more than I did before I even started The Orange Rhino Challenge . . . and it was all self-inflicted. I put so much pressure on myself to succeed that I was crumbling at every hard moment.

"Orange Rhino! Orange Rhino! Orange Rhino!" James and Edward shouted with smiles and such excitement that I practically had to yell to get them to stop. They love games, love them! In fact, one of their favorite games, much to my dismay, is yelling out names to each other, their most favorite names being butthead, stinky butt, smelly face, fart face, and booger nose. Glamorous and loving, eh?! But seriously, I have no idea why I hadn't thought to use their favorite game to my advantage before!

"Orange Rhino" very quickly became the new favorite game in the house, and not just because it was played a lot (eh hem, at least once an hour during the first two weeks it was created), but also because we all loved it for different reasons. My boys loved it because it gave them a chance to "call me out" as I do to them for "questionable behavior" and, of course, because it kept me from yelling. I loved it because my boys were so gosh darn good at it and it really helped me to stop yelling during intense times.

You know, I would have thought that as such an "experienced" yeller, I would have been an expert at predicting when a yell was coming and knowing when I needed to remove myself from tough situations. Alas, clearly I was not. My kids, however, were, and continue to be, complete experts at predicting my yells. Just as they have sixth senses about when I need a hug or a kiss to feel better, they have sixth senses as to when I am about to blow it. I am sure that my eyes start widening, my eyebrows start rising, and my feet start stomping. I am sure that there are many other signs that indeed only my kids would know because they are the ones able to actually see them and witness them. And this is why they were the perfect people to ask to help me stop yelling.

If you had told me at the beginning of the challenge that my children would be some of the biggest aids in my ability to actually stop yelling, I wouldn't have believed you. My kids, a help to stop yelling? You mean the people that drive me to yell? I mean sure, they are my inspiration to stop yelling, and looking at them and their beautiful faces should be enough to stop me. But sadly, sometimes, they weren't. But oh, oh, when my boys say, "Orange Rhino, Mommy!" it stops me dead in my tracks. Every. Single. Time. It is a double whammy—sweet faces reminding me of my promise and even sweeter, persistent, yet encouraging and sometimes desperate voices reminding me to calm down and speak with love, not anger.

I always expected that I would be the one helping my kids in life and that I would help them stay on track to achieve their goals. I never in a thousand years thought that my kids would help me achieve a goal, especially not at such young ages. And yet, here I am, feeling confident that I owe much of my success to my kids and their enthusiastic embracing of The Orange Rhino game. And here I am feeling confident that when people ask me, "Did you tell your kids? Do you think they should know?" that answering with a resounding YES is definitely the right answer.

I have been asked in the past if telling my kids to say "Orange Rhino" made them overuse it and take advantage of the situation, such as, "Let's say 'Orange Rhino' when we are really naughty so Mommy can't yell at us and we don't get in trouble." My answer? Yes, there were definitely times my kids tried to pull this stunt! And, yes, I didn't yell. But that doesn't mean I let the behavior slide. Nope, even without yelling I still did make it clear that their behavior was unacceptable and that I was still angry at the action. I also reminded them that the purpose of The Orange Rhino game is to help me not yell, which is a benefit to them; for that to happen, they had to use it properly.

Orange Rhino Revelations

- My sons are around me all the time; they are an awesome and always available support group! Plus, they have the perfect view to notice any visual cues that I am close to yelling.

- Asking my kids for help doesn't diminish my role as a parent. It teaches them how to ask for help and instills the sense of empowerment and confidence all kids crave.

Today's Actions

- **Teach your children The Orange Rhino game.** Ask your kids if they know off-hand of any visual signs of when you are going to yell. Ask them what the signs look like. Practice yelling and having them "Orange Rhino" you when they see the signs.

- **Make an Orange Rhino sign.** Cut out the large Orange Rhino on the cover flap. Write your own motivational statement on it. Attach it with tape to a stick of sorts (Popsicle stick, chopstick, skewer). Place it where everyone can see it and instruct kids to grab it and hold it up in "Orange Rhino" needed moments!

> **66** **The parents exist to teach the child,**
> but also they must learn what
> the child has to teach them; and the child has
> a very great deal to teach them. **99**
>
> —Arnold Bennett

Today's Tips

COOL	Say positive thoughts about your kids out loud; it forces you to focus on the good behaviors, which inspires kids to act well.
WARM	Embrace your inner teacher. Say, "1, 2, 3, look at me" or ring a bell.
HOT	Start clapping; if you're angry and you know it, clap your hands! This is a great stress reliever.

**DON'T YELL!
Remember your
Promise to your kids!**

Edward loved using this sign so much that he insisted we make several: one for the kitchen, one for the boys' bathroom, one for my bedroom, and on and on and on!

Day 4

Practice Yelling "Away" from Kids: I Love Yelling into Toilets

I started The Orange Rhino Challenge with no idea how I was going to not yell. I mean, I knew I would need more patience to keep it together, more sleep to get said patience, and more ice cream at the end of the day to unwind from all the stress of learning to be more patient. But beyond that, I didn't know how I would physically stop a yell. I mean, yelling was practically a natural instinct when I felt frustrated. Ironically, it turned out that just as much as my body naturally yelled, it also naturally took the first small step to stop yelling.

It was a normal morning in Orange Rhino Land. You know, all my boys slept in, then made their beds, got dressed, and brushed their teeth without being asked. Then they quietly tiptoed into my room to wake me up and bring me the breakfast and coffee that the elves had made while I slept. Afterward, they so peacefully played together without incident. Ah, yes. It was absolutely wonderful.

Of course, then I woke up and realized I was dreaming and that it was indeed a real normal morning in Orange Rhino Land, one where I had stayed up too late the night before cleaning the house. Ha! Who am I kidding! I stayed up too late reading People.com for the latest celebrity gossip, which meant this morning I was wiped and didn't want to get out of bed. At. All. My alarm went off at 5:30 that morning to make sure that I got up, showered, and got mentally awake and prepared for the day to begin. Instead of getting up, I whacked the alarm with all my might and went back to sleep. Bad move. Bad, bad move; like really bad way to start one of my early days of my no-yelling challenge.

If I am not totally awake, with it, and energized before my boys loudly charge in saying, "GOOD MORNING" followed by a chorus of "My toy" and "He broke my LEGOs" and "Is it the weekend? I don't want to go to school," then my patience isn't totally awake either. And for that matter, neither is my tolerance for noise, my desire to field thousands of questions, or my ability to manage all the chaos the morning brings without wanting to just scream!

So that morning when my three energetic, loud, and "we-got-lots-of-sleep-and-are-WIDE-awake" boys ran into my room to wake up their "I-didn't-get-enough-sleep-and-I-am-still-very-much-asleep" mom and started the morning onslaught of complaints, questions, concerns, and loud yippees, I replied with, **"Mommy isn't ready to be a parent yet this morning. I am going back to sleep."**

As if I got to go back to sleep! They all pounced on the bed, pushing my patience, tolerance, and coping skills back into deeper slumber. On cue, I heard Mac crying on the monitor, forcing me to get out of bed and stumble down the hall to get him. Bleary-eyed, I got him dressed while his brothers ran up and down the hall, exhibiting just how awake they were and proving just how much I still wanted to be sleeping, dreaming of a quiet morning. I stumbled back down the hall to get myself dressed.

As Mac played at my feet while I picked out clothes for the day, I reminded myself about my Orange Rhino Challenge. I reminded myself that I needed to get it together and wake up, quickly, or I could kiss Day 3 goodbye before the clock even struck 7:00. Then I realized *quick* wasn't fast enough.

Six feet thundered down the hall and stomped into my room. Six eyes looked at me bawling. Three hands flew through the air pointing fingers and three mouths screamed at the top of their lungs, "Mommmmmmm! Mommyyyyy! Mama!"

"He hit me."

"He started it."

"Ow. Ow."

The intensity of the screams and the bickering was just too much to bear for my still half-asleep mind. I so had no desire to deal with this situation. I just had the desire to scream, *"GO AWAY! BE QUIET! PLEASE!"* But before I could do that, without even knowing what I was doing, I turned, put my head into my hanging clothes, and just let out a good, ol'-fashioned yell.

"Arghhhhhhhhhhhhh!" I bellowed.

"Oh sh*t," I immediately thought to myself. *"I totally just yelled. Does that count? I mean I didn't yell at my son; but I yelled. But I didn't yell mean words, I just let off some steam. I am good, right?"*

I slowly and nervously removed my head from my ten-year-old sweater sets and turned to look at my kids, scared to see their response. I knew if they looked scared, were crying, or opened their mouths to tell me how awful I was that I had blown it. I had been trying so hard to not yell and had already gone two days. I felt proud and just wasn't ready to feel failure or disappointment.

Everyone had stopped crying. They just looked at me. Stared, really.

Edward spoke first. "Mommy, that was silly. You just put your head in the closet and yelled at your clothes!"

I spoke next. "Um, guys, did I just yell? Do I have to start over?" I asked nervously.

James, my very serious and logical child, put his finger on his chin, twitched his lip, and rolled his eyes. This was his pondering face. "Well, Mom ...," he started. *"Uh oh, so not good,"* I thought.

"No, you're fine. You didn't yell AT us. You yelled at your clothes. Which is okay."

"Yeah, yeah," chimed in Edward.

"But did I hurt your feelings? Did I scare you?" I asked very intently. These were and continue to be two important reasons I stopped yelling. I simply did not want to scare my children anymore or intentionally hurt their feelings.

"Nope. You made me laugh," smiled Edward.

"Are you sure?" I implored. Even though I felt that what I did was okay, that what I did wasn't mean or directed at them and that it truly was just letting off some steam in a more managed way so it wasn't hurtful, I still wanted their opinion. Again, at the end of the day, my boys are my audience. They are my best and most important judges.

James interrupted my doubting thoughts with reassuring ones. "We're totally sure, Mom. We're The Orange Rhino Police, you know. We watch to see if you break the law. And we say you are fine," James firmly stated.

And with that, The Orange Rhino Police were born and I got a free pass.

And with that, just as fast as they ran in, they ran off to the basement yelling, "Let's get on our police clothes and badges!"

And with that, I was totally awake—awakened not by their yelling and fighting, or my "yelling," but by the fact that I couldn't stop smiling. I just loved how into The Orange Rhino Challenge they were and how supportive they were trying to be.

> Inanimate objects don't have feelings, kids do. My clothes won't cry if I yell at them, my kids will. The waffles in the freezer won't get scared if I yell at them, my kids will. The toilet won't scream at me, "You're the worst person ever!" if I yell into it, my kids will.

And I loved that I had just discovered a new way to manage a yell when I was past the point of stopping it: releasing it into an inanimate object instead of at my kids. When I felt a yell coming, I could turn and let out an "ARGHHH" or an "AHHHH" into a closet-type thing, such as a trash can, freezer, closet, drawer, or purse. Inanimate objects don't have feelings, kids do. My clothes won't cry if I yell at them, my kids will. The waffles in the freezer won't get scared if I yell at them, my kids will. The toilet won't scream at me, "You're the worst person ever!" if I yell into it, my kids will.

I didn't let the mean words out, just the frustration. After a few days of doing that, and a few days of my kids laughing at me for yelling at my clothes, I realized that I could indeed control myself. The next step was to not let out the AHHHH. **The more I practiced controlling where I directed my yells, the more I learned how to calm myself down so that the yell didn't need to come out at all.** Indeed, as the English footballer Bobby Robson says, "Practice makes permanent." (Which, by the way, is a saying I much prefer to "practice makes perfect." Who needs perfection?!)

Yes, I know. It sounds crazy. And silly. And outright ridiculous. But it worked that morning and so many times in the early days when I was still learning how to not yell, how to recognize a brewing yell and stop it, and how to stay calm(er) throughout the day, so that trying moments like that morning didn't push me to the point of needing to scream to feel better.

Besides, I would rather yell into a toilet any day of the week than yell at my kids. That is, if the toilet doesn't smell from being covered in pee and having several floaters in it that weren't flushed down. Yep, been there, done that. BLECH! I was in such a rush to get to the bathroom and let a yell out that I forgot to look before I put my head down. Ooops. But hey, I didn't forget to stop myself, turn away from my boys and the infuriating moment, and yell away from them, so it was all good. I flushed down all the crap—figuratively and literally—and walked out of the bathroom renewed. A little disgusted from my face being so close to poop? Yeah. But not disgusted with myself for keeping it together. Oh, yeah!

Day 4: Revelations, Actions, and Tips

Orange Rhino Revelations
- **I can't always control my kids' actions, but I can always choose to control my reaction.**
- **I can always choose to walk away, take a deep breath, or yell into a toilet instead of yelling at them.**
- Baby steps are big steps; turning and yelling away felt silly and small at first, but that small step was a huge, 180-degree change in behavior.

Today's Actions
- **Practice turning away.** Even if the yell still slips out and is still words, turning away is still a step. Turning away still stops the words from going directly from your mouth to your kids' eyes and hearts. If you can, when you turn away, find a silly inanimate object to yell into. The upside to this? (a) It can be funny and stop kids in their tracks, (b) it helps you regain control, and (c) it gives you a way to still let the frustration out.

- **Count the number of times you have to turn away to yell.** Why? First, it is an eye-opener and a motivator that change needs to happen. Second, it is a great way to measure progress! At the end of this book you can count again and see how much you are yelling less!

I realize that yelling into a toilet or a purse might seem silly and embarrassing at times, and I fully acknowledge that there are some better ways to let frustration out. You will learn those ways in due time. But right now, let's focus on realizing that you do have more control than you might have thought. This will give you the much-needed self-confidence that you can do this!

> **❝ The journey of a thousand miles**
> begins with a single step. **❞**
>
> —Lao Tzu

Today's Tips

COOL	Gently pull your fingers throughout the day to release tension; for what it's worth, someone told me the middle finger releases the most tension. Ha!
WARM	Splash cold water on your face; this snaps you right out of a bad mood.
	Text a frustrated message to a friend so you can clear your mind enough to then send a warm and loving one to your child.
HOT	Yell into a closet; remember, clothes don't have feelings, but kids do.

Day 5

Surround Yourself with Reminders:
Orange Is the New Gray

I will never forget the day in seventh grade when I tried to emulate Julia Roberts. My parents *finally* let me watch *Pretty Woman*, and I instantly fell in love with Julia's (Vivian's) wardrobe. Okay, the fancy, more sophisticated one—not the one she wore, um, walking about. The red dress for the opera? Loved, loved, loved it! But what I loved most? The black blazer over the white shirt. I just loved it—so much so that the Monday morning after seeing the movie, I stole one of my dad's black blazers and wore it to school. Now, it was too cold to wear a white T-shirt (and I think I was still too shy to wear one for fear of my bra showing, gasp!), so instead I paired it with a navy and red striped turtleneck. Yeah, looking back, so not a fashionable outfit. Um, where were The Orange Rhino fashion police when I needed them? Ha! But I didn't care. I thought I looked awesome and soooo ahead of the curve.

No one else at school thought so, or so it seemed, because no one said, "Hey, cool jacket." Fast-forward one day. The most popular girl in school comes in wearing, wouldn't you know it, her dad's black blazer and a turtleneck. And wouldn't you know it, everyone told her how awesome she looked and how cool the look was. Eh hem, I wore the same look yesterday?! Where do you think she got it?! Fast-forward another day and another ... every girl it seemed was coming in wearing different blazers. For the first time, and the last time, I had started a fashion trend (kind of), and if you know me, this is not only practically impossible, but also outright hilarious.

You see, I am the exact opposite of being on-trend. I have no fashion sense or intuition, especially now that I am home with my boys. I am lucky if my jeans aren't ripped and are the "right" color blue. I have been wearing the same belt for eight years and have no plans to replace it. My hair is always in a braid even though supposedly only tween girls wear braids. I don't accessorize or know how to, and I really am not that into clothes shopping. Every time I need to get dressed up for something, I have to call a girlfriend for either a purse or an entire outfit. And I am okay with all of this. It is who I am and being "on-trend" doesn't really matter to me.

Well, it didn't matter to me until Spring Season 2012, that is.

When I picked the color orange for my rhino symbol, I just picked it because I liked the symbolism—warmth, energy, determination, encouragement, happiness, and success. I didn't pick it hoping it was an on-trend color; I picked it because it was the perfect color for the Orange Rhino Challenge. Orange so wonderfully encapsulated what I wanted and needed. I wanted to be more warm and happy and successful. I needed energy, determination, and encouragement to do so. *Voilà!* Orange Rhino.

It was late January when I decided on orange, so the spring colors hadn't really sprung out yet. Fast-forward a few weeks, and wouldn't you know it, the popular color, the color that was everywhere? Orange! And the most popular combination? Orange and pink—my blog colors. It was surreal. Anywhere I shopped, whether it was for household supplies (orange potholders, anyone?) or spring clothes (orange shirts, shorts, bathing suits, hats), orange screamed at me—nicely, of course. Orange was totally the new black. I was totally on-trend, and it totally mattered to me. But not because it made me cool, but because it made my challenge easier!

How so? Well, for one thing, crazy or not, I kind of felt like the world was conspiring to support me in my challenge, which gave me even more strength. Obviously, the fashion world didn't plan its entire season in anticipation of little ol' me and my promise to my kids. But still, it was so wonderful to go to stores with my kids and see orange everywhere rooting for me saying, "Hey girl, you can do this! Are the kids throwing a temper tantrum in aisle 9? No problem! Look to your left at the beautiful orange and pink scarves or look to the right at the orange necklaces."

Being surrounded by visual reminders to parent with more love and warmth kept me on my toes and focused on my goal.

Being "on-trend" and seeing orange items everywhere inspired me to surround myself with visual orange reminders to stay on track. This made it infinitely easier to remember my promise. I just couldn't resist the scarves or the necklaces, the orange shirts for the boys or the ones for me, the orange pens for writing school notes or the super awesome orange spatula that says, "This Kitchen Is Seasoned with Love." Um, perfect! It was all perfect: Now I had perfect little ways to surround myself with orange at home and on the go to remember my promise to be warm and loving.

My husband might say that I went a little overboard with the orange shopping. I would obviously disagree (okay, I would only disagree a little). But it was fantastic. On mornings when I woke up not rested, I either put on an orange shirt or an orange necklace. If my orange clothes weren't clean, or if one boy was especially, um, passionate that morning, I had him wear orange. There were days that started so dismal that within five minutes of getting downstairs to start breakfast I had already marched everyone back upstairs to put orange clothes on. I kid you not.

I also, kid you not, that it worked. It really, really worked. Being surrounded by visual reminders to parent with more love and warmth kept me on my toes and focused on my goal. Especially the orange clothing—it is hard not to remember your promise when you move your arm to open the fridge for the umpteenth time that morning and a long orange object (my arm) swings in front of your face. It is as if my clothes would say to me, "Hey, lady, don't yell at your kids for being 'loud' just because you feel flustered from running late and can't seem to focus enough to remember that you need to pack lunches."

It's funny, when my husband started dating me, he often said, "Do you own any clothes with color—you know, beyond black and gray?"

My answer? "Yes, I have lots of navy blues and whites. And some dark pink. But color, what do you mean by color?"

"Green. Yellow. Orange. Anything," he replied.

Well, twelve years and counting later, his tune has changed. He now asks, "Do you own any clothes that aren't orange?!"

My answer? "No, not really."

Orange is so my new black, and I love it. I love that the majority of my shirts are shades of orange and pink, and not just because of the irony, or because it turns out that orange is a good color on me, but because wearing orange clothes truly helped me remember my promise to yell less. Frank Sinatra was right when he said, "Orange is the happiest color." I don't look at orange and frown; I look at it and smile, thinking of how grateful I am that I am surrounded everywhere by orange gatekeepers! Because that is what the color orange does for me now—it acts as my much-needed gatekeeper. The Arabian proverb powerfully states: "The words of the tongue should have three gatekeepers: is it true, is it kind, is it necessary?" Orange definitely reminds my mind to stop so that my tongue only says things that are true, kind, and necessary and most definitely doesn't yell anything that is the opposite!

As soon as I realized just how powerful the orange visual reminders were, I did do just a teensy, eensy, weensy little bit more shopping. This time, however, I went with intention. I went to a beauty store to buy orange nail polish and painted my toes. What better way to start the day off on the right foot than seeing orange on your toes in the shower or when you get dressed? And I went to an office supplies store and bought orange sticky notes to put in high-stress areas, such as the kids' backpacks, the bathroom mirror, and the front dash of the car.

Now, who knows how long orange is going to stay popular as a color or how long everyday useful physical reminders will be readily available in orange. And who knows, maybe orange really wasn't on-trend as I thought it was. Maybe it was just on-trend to me because I needed it to be, because I sought support from anything and any source. The good news is that as I realized the power of having a visual cue to stop yelling, I naturally started seeing orange everywhere, and not just in the "hot looks of the season" areas.

There are orange foods (carrots, oranges, cheese); orange construction signs ("Go Slow," um, perfect reminder for life and parenting with more patience); orange logos (Dunkin' Donuts, anyone?); and orange leaves and flowers. These are great natural reminders when kids are stepping on each other's toes walking to school. There was and is orange anywhere I look for it when I need it to remind me to Yell Less and Love More; for that, it is so my new favorite color. Yes, orange is my new black!

Or should I say, orange is the new gray? Yeah, that makes more sense. Regular rhinos—you know, the ones that charge when provoked? They are gray. I am so over being a gray rhino and charging with my voice; I am all about being a calmer Orange Rhino. Yep, orange is the new gray in more ways than one!

Day 5: Revelations, Actions, and Tips

Orange Rhino Revelations

- Orange objects not only served as phenomenal reminders of my promise to be warmer, by they also gave me something to focus on so I could regain a sense of calm when I wanted to yell.

- Orange support existed all around me at all times; I just needed to push myself to look for it and seek it when I needed it.

Today's Actions

- **Find at least one orange item that you can use as a reminder to stop yelling.** Ideas: clothes, sticky notes, Play-Doh, construction paper, this book.... If you have time and resources, consider doing some light shopping. If you can only get one thing, I suggest sticky notes because they are economical and can go anywhere and everywhere!

- **Place your orange item(s) in high-yelling zones.** Popular spots for placement: bathroom, front dashboard in the car, where backpacks hang, and bedroom doors. If you do use sticky notes, write quick notes to self: You can do it!

I know that orange isn't everyone's favorite color and that some people really can't stand it. I kind of felt that way too, until I fell in love with the symbolism of orange. So give orange a chance and you might come to love it too. Besides, I learned after the fact that orange is a great color for getting attention without being harsh (red), and getting attention is definitely what we are going after here!

Me, the morning after back-to-school night:

James, I couldn't guess which worksheet was yours. I thought your favorite color was red and no sheets listed that color. I finally found yours, though—it was the last one on the table. When did orange become your favorite color?

James:

Oh, I love orange now because The Orange Rhino keeps you from yelling.

Today's Tips

COOL 😐	Paint your nails—toes and fingers—orange; this reminds you to be warm and composed.
WARM 😣	Tell yourself, "I won't yell. I won't yell. I won't yell," over and over again until the moment has passed.
HOT 😫	**Orange Rhino Favorite:** Grab your children and hug them. Instead of creating a tug-of-war with my kids when we disagree, I start a hug-of-love; everyone calms down and refocuses, and what better reminder to yell less than to hug your kiddos?

2

Gain Awareness

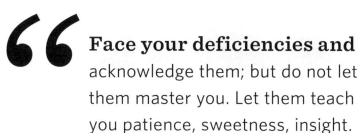

Face your deficiencies and acknowledge them; but do not let them master you. Let them teach you patience, sweetness, insight.

—Helen Keller

I affectionately call this chapter "The chapter that everyone really, really needs to read, but doesn't want to read!" Here we talk about the core of learning to yell less: tracking your triggers. Ugh. I know. "Tracking triggers" sounds like work; that's because it is work. And it sounds time-consuming. That's because it is time-consuming. But you know what else it is? An absolutely powerful and necessary tool. Learning about my triggers quickly gave me concrete insights and ideas on how to start successfully managing my desire to yell. From tracking, I taught myself how to master my triggers instead of letting them master me. Did learning about my triggers make me uncomfortable? Absolutely. Acknowledging that I had a big, ugly deficiency in the parenting bucket isn't exactly something that I would like to do every day, for this realization rocked me to the core. But tracking triggers, well, this rocked me to the core in a whole new way because what I learned made my life quieter, calmer, happier, and easier, too!

Day 6

Start Tracking Triggers:
Love at Second Sight

When I met my husband on a blind date thirteen years ago, it was definitely not love at first sight. I thought he was a pompous a** and wanted nothing to do with him. He, however, thought I was worthy of another date and tried desperately to get my number. I, on the other hand, tried desperately to pull every excuse out of the book to not give him my number.

"I don't have a pen and paper," I said stubbornly.

"Oh, but I have my phone; I can save it there," he said unfazed.

"Oh, right. You know, I really feel like I am going to throw up. I had Benny T's pizza for dinner and it just ain't sitting. I need to go home now."

"Benny T's pizza? Oh, I totally get it. Can I walk you, then?" he offered graciously.

"No, I live a block away, I'm fine," I said less graciously.

And then his buddy called him, he turned his head, and I shot out of that bar as fast as I could. Later that weekend I realized how close-minded I had been and decided to call him. One week later we had our second date and it was totally love at second sight! On that date, I determined that I had been totally wrong in my opinion of him and that furthermore he was the man I would marry someday. I just knew it. One week later, I found myself finally inspired to lose the extra 40 pounds (18 kg) I had put on in college. I wanted to be healthy enough to spend a long life with my future husband; I wanted to be able to run after our kids together and play with them without tiring out! Driven by my heartfelt desire to change, the next day I joined my friend on her diet and did what she did: I wrote down what I ate for a couple of weeks.

Oh, how I hated having to remember to write everything down, having to find a pen and my paper and then having to admit that I had just overindulged in Ben & Jerry's ice cream ... again! It was such a pain and I felt so incompetent! But then, well, then I slowly started to warm up to the idea because tracking what I ate and seeing how much I overate (um, can we say nighttime cupboard raids when bored...) not only motivated me to work even harder to cut back but also showed me where I needed to focus to cut back. I went from hating tracking my eating habits to loving it, as I loved that I finally had a concrete map on how to lose weight! It was love at second sight!

Well, guess what? Not only did I lose the weight, but I also gained confidence, pride, and more happiness.

Guess what else? **When I stopped yelling, I also lost weight. Emotional weight. I lost guilt, sadness, frustration, and disappointment, and I also gained confidence, pride, and more happiness.**

I credit a lot of my losing said emotional weight to doing exactly what I did when I lost my real weight—that is, I tracked my yelling habits. The only difference was this time around I didn't track what wonderful thing went into my mouth, but instead I tracked what not-so-wonderful thought wanted to come out.

When I started tracking, I had no idea whether the tool that helped me lose weight would help me stop yelling, but I just had to try it because I had no other really concrete game plan. Nope, none at all. I hadn't read any books on the matter, so I just assumed—okay really, really, REALLY hoped—that if I worked really hard, bit my tongue a lot, stumbled along as I figured out alternatives to yelling besides biting my tongue, and texted friends in times I needed support, then I would, you know, miraculously stop yelling.

Knowing this wasn't necessarily the most sustainable plan, I added the tracking piece. I desperately hoped that, as when I lost 40 pounds (18 kg) by tracking my eating habits, tracking my yelling habits would help me lose my dependence on yelling as a means of parenting. Oh, how I hoped that seeing on paper all the times I wanted to yell would scare me enough and open my eyes enough to motivate me to keep working hard to not yell.

Oh, how I hoped that maybe, just maybe, it would help me see which areas I needed to work on the hardest, and therefore, would finally help me kiss yelling goodbye.

I wrote down on orange (obviously) sticky notes for about two weeks any time I wanted to yell, why I wanted to yell, who I wanted to yell at, where I was when I wanted to yell, and how I felt before I wanted to yell. And then I wrote down any other tidbits of information that I thought might be useful. I found some of my notes the other day while cleaning up my desk. These are some—yes, some—of my favorites. Because I used to yell a lot, I had a lot of notes to read through!

> *"Day 2. 7:54 a.m. James woke at 5:00, woke Edward. Andrew then got scared and screamed and woke Mac. So tired can't function. Want to scream at every sound."*
> *"Day 4. 5:42 p.m. Wow. James spilled milk at dinner. Then used plate as surfboard while I changed Mac's diaper. Are you kidding me? Serenity now."*
> *"Day 4. 6:17 p.m. Sat down to pee. Seat and walls and floor covered in pee. ARGHHHHHH!"*
> *"Day 5. 11:48 a.m. Gonna scream. There are toys everywhere I step. I hate clutter!"*
> *"Day ? 8:53 a.m. Actually got kids in car for school without yelling. Miracle."*

At first, tracking my yelling was a brutal experience, and not just because it took a lot of time and commitment, but also because of the results. Seeing on paper just how many times I actually wanted to yell was nothing short of an absolutely sobering experience. It turned out that I wanted to yell a lot more than I thought I did, which meant one thing: My problem was bigger than I originally thought. Ouch.

Yes, I didn't just want to yell when we were trying to get to school or during bath time. It turned out that I also wanted to yell anytime I stepped on a toy, anytime the kids ran around me during meal preparation, anytime the kids didn't fully pick up the basement, anytime I felt tired or hungry, anytime the kids felt tired or hungry and therefore whined and whined and did I mention, whine?!

Yes, it turned out that I had a lot more "problem areas," or triggers, than I thought I did, and yes, it hurt (okay, sucked) to realize that. BUT, I soon saw the beauty in my newfound awareness. As hoped, my "plan" of writing down when I wanted to yell had actually worked. As I perused my notes after a few days, it became clear that there was a strong pattern of when and why I yelled. Knowing which times of day and which situations tempted me to yell meant that I could actually prepare for those moments so that I didn't yell during them.

Simply stated, my awareness of my yelling triggers created an awesome mental alarm system that would stop me before I yelled. With my triggers in my mind, anytime one dared to tempt me, this little Orange Rhino in my head would go, *"Warning. Warning. Toys are on the floor. You know this means you could yell. Prepare. Take a deep breath."*

Or ...

As I perused my notes after a few days, it became clear that there was a strong pattern of when and why I yelled. Knowing which times of day and which situations tempted me to yell meant that I could actually prepare for those moments so that I didn't yell during them.

"Warning. Warning. You are tired. Exercise now or yell later. Drop and do ten push-ups now."

Or …

"Warning. Warning. You are running late to school. You will probably yell. Start talking positive thoughts to yourself now so that you don't yell."

That last little warning comment always makes me laugh because whenever I do say that to myself, I already am talking to myself! But hey, whatever works, right? Well, tracking triggers, my friends, works. Trust me, it really, really works, and I am totally in love and committed to this tool! Did I love this tool when I first started using it? Heck, no! But as soon as I realized how useful it was, how much it helped me focus and feel less overwhelmed by the enormity of learning to stop yelling, I fell head over heels in love with the tool—totally love at second sight and totally worth putting all your heart and soul into doing.

Orange Rhino Revelations

- Tracking my triggers took time and effort up front, but made life easier in the long term.
- Tracking my triggers gave me a road map to stop yelling.

Today's Actions

- **Start tracking your triggers.** The goal is collecting information, not solving problems. All the information you collect will help you gain insight into what changes you can make, both within yourself and within your environment, to yell less. There is a sample trigger tracking sheet and some blank ones for your use in the Resources section (see page 198).

- **Record every time you yell.** If you didn't yell but wanted to, record that too, and note what kept you from yelling!

  Be detailed: Fill out as many boxes as you can. The more information you collect, the more you will learn and the better you will be able to tackle your triggers. Even small details you think may be irrelevant may be relevant when you look back at four days of tracking.

  Be truthful: Don't skip recording tough moments because it hurts to see the truth on paper. I know this will be hard because no one wants to see those times officially recorded; but, trust me, it is those hardest times to record where you can learn the most.

  Be committed: Keep recording throughout the day. It will be tempting to stop after a few episodes because you might feel you have enough. Keep going. The goal is to see trends, and again, the more info, the better! Added bonus? You can write out frustration instead of yelling!

Seeing how often you yell can be discouraging, understandably. Be kind to yourself and remember that you are gathering this tough information so that you can learn from it and teach yourself to change.

> **66** **The only real mistake is the** one from which we learn nothing. **99**
>
> —John Powell

Today's Tips

COOL	**Orange Rhino Favorite:** Place orange sticky notes all over the house, especially in areas where you are apt to yell; when you don't yell, write down a positive note, such as "I did it!" and put it up to encourage you.
WARM	**Orange Rhino Favorite:** Raise two hands in the air; this gets kids' attention and acts as a warning that you are about to blow; it also forces you to stretch, which can be calming.
HOT	Find a piece of paper and crumple it up over and over and over again until calm.

Postpone your yells with a Post-it Party!

Day 7

Be Honest with Yourself: "Why, Mommy, Why, Why?"

Just two weeks before my blind date with my hubby, I sat at my kitchen table across from Mike, a guy I had been casually dating for about four months. Even though he was a great guy with a great career, he felt more like a great friend than a potential serious boyfriend. Anywho, that night, as he talked nervously about wanting to take me as his girlfriend to a family party, I fidgeted with my chopsticks, trying to figure out how to let him know that I didn't really want girlfriend status. I then put my chopsticks down and cracked open a fortune cookie that read, I kid you not, "You are surrounded by great friends."

Mike asked me what my fortune said. I didn't have the guts to read it out loud because I knew I had an awful poker face, so I gently slid it across the table. He read it, took one look at my face, and knew what I was thinking.

"You just want to be friends, don't you?"

"Yes, I am so sorry."

I then started in with all sorts of lines—lies, actually—because that felt easier (and kinder) than telling the truth. First I told him I didn't want to be in a serious relationship, but um, eh hem, I met my husband two weeks later! Then I said, and I remember saying this as if it were yesterday, "It's not you, it's me." Oh, oh, that line was so easy to say at the time; it felt right even though it was a lie. Oh, it felt so easy to lie then.

Fast-forward elevenish years to the first few months of The Orange Rhino Challenge. I started tracking triggers with three main assumptions: that it would motivate me, that it would identify triggers to work on, and that the triggers would all be because of my kids and never, ever because of me. Well, the first two assumptions were spot-on; the third, not so much. Actually, it wasn't even close. **I learned early on that most of the time it was me, and not my kids, who was at the root of my desire to yell.** I begrudgingly, but much more so gratefully, thank Andrew for helping me to see that, for helping me understand that **"It's not you, it's me"** isn't just a line to use to break up with someone, but also to break up with yelling.

One morning when I felt especially grumpy and impatient, Andrew started hammering me incessantly and insistently with questions such as, "Why is the sky blue?" "Why do light bulbs light up?" "Why do tractors not have more wheels?" and "Why does it rain?" As usual, I didn't know the answers to any of his questions and tried my best to give a good response. And as usual he felt unsatisfied and started asking me, "But why, Mommy, why, why?" until he got an answer that felt right. After a few rounds of questioning, I as usual just wanted to incessantly and insistently yell at him, *"Why are you asking me so many questions?! Why? Why? Why?!"* I didn't yell this but oh, oh did I speak it rather abruptly. Andrew responded sweetly, "But why, why, you mad Mommy, why?"

Shoot, yet another question I didn't know the answer to! But this time, I didn't respond with a half-assed answer to his question. I couldn't respond halfheartedly; it just didn't feel right. So, I embraced his question and without even realizing it, I started imitating him. I found myself saying, "Why, Sheila, Why? Why? WHY?"

"Why do you want to yell?" I asked myself. "Is it because of all the questions?"

"Yes. I can't stand the nonstop questioning," I replied to myself.

"Really? That's ridiculous. You want to yell because your son is curious?" I asked myself.

"Yes!" I replied back.

But that answer didn't sit at all; it felt awful saying that I wanted to yell because of my son's wonderful curiosity, so I started again with my own incessant and insistent questioning.

"Why, Sheila, why do you really want to yell? Why?" I asked myself.

"Just because," I replied, using one of my favorite answers to my kids. I always hoped it would stop their never-ending question sessions. Of course it doesn't work for my kids, and it didn't work for me. My gut still unsatisfied and unsettled, I started again.

"Why, Sheila, WHY?"

"ARGH. I don't know.... Maybe because I am exhausted and can't focus. Because I have 1,001 things to do right now and answering questions has lost its cuteness. I want to give a good answer, but I also really want to just yell, 'ENOUGH ALREADY!'"

"So, again WHY do you want to yell? Because of the questions or because of your own bad mood and inability to be patient?"

> I didn't want to believe that I could take out my own anger on my kids. I didn't want to believe that oftentimes my yelling was my fault and not my kid's fault, that I yelled at my boys not really because of them, but because of me, because I was in a bad place.

And then, my mind stopped. I knew that I had finally uncovered the truth, the real truth, because I felt an undeniable sense of clarity in my gut. I no longer desired to ask "Why?" because my mind said, "Uh-huh, I got it. I don't want to yell because of the questions. I want to yell because my issues are making me super impatient. Shoot, it's not him, it's me."

The truth stung and I struggled to accept it. Elevenish years had passed since I said to Mike, "It's not you, it's me," and the line that had so easily slipped off my tongue years prior, I now found near impossible to say.

Why did I struggle to say, "It's not you that's making me yell; it's me making me yell?" Why, oh why? Because I just didn't want to believe that I could be unnecessarily causing my kids pain. I didn't want to believe that I could take out my own anger on my kids. I didn't want to believe that oftentimes my yelling was my fault and not my kids' fault, that I yelled at my boys not really because of them, but because of me, because I was in a bad place.

It's not you taking too long to tie your shoes that's making me want to yell ... it's me. I am mad at myself for surfing Facebook, causing us to run late.

It's not you coming joyfully and loudly into my bedroom to wake me that's making me want to yell … it's me. I am angry with your father for something he said.

It's not you refusing to eat your lunch that's making me want to yell … it's me. I am frustrated with the insurance agency for not paying our bills.

Oh the list goes on and on and on of things my kids supposedly "did" to push me to yell, but really, they didn't push me to yell, they didn't make me yell. I made me yell. My bad mood pushed me to yell. My inability to handle my stress pushed me to yell. My refusal to take ownership of my role in the "yelling game" pushed me to yell. Sure, my kids' behavior at times is annoying and frustrating and maddening and it can entice me to yell, but I realized that morning that my behavior needs just as much scrutiny and attention as theirs. When I own my mood, when I control my mood, I am much more able to control my patience and ability to not yell at them unnecessarily.

Up to this point in my journey, I had focused all my energy on changing my kids' behavior and coming up with calming ways to respond when they frustrated me. This approach worked really well—really, really well. But it was exhausting because a lot of the time, when they behaved beautifully and acted as one would expect kids to act, I still found myself frustrated with them and wanting to yell at them for no apparent reason. In not looking at and owning my own behavior, I created unnecessary work for myself.

It took me a while to fully embrace this fact, that if I worked on managing my mood and understanding my role in things, then I wouldn't have to spend so much energy not yelling, but wow, once I did, once I started making a habit of regularly looking at my own behavior, the challenge truly got easier. **Anytime I found myself working extra hard to keep it together I knew it was time to stop looking outward at my kids' behavior and start looking inward at my own; I knew it was time to ask "Why, Sheila, why, why?" until my gut became satisfied with the "it's me" truth.** Yes, working to get the truth and then acknowledging it was hard, but the truth made it easy to stop myself from yelling unnecessarily by giving me the clarity and confidence to focus my frustration where it belonged, by saying to myself, *"Don't yell at them. You aren't mad at them, you are mad at something else."*

There are days when it's hard to ask "Why, why, why?" and when it would be much easier and faster to blame the kids or to have a fortune cookie tell me the real trigger and how to solve it. But I don't have the luxury of fortune cookies telling me how to not yell and I don't have the heart to blame and yell at my kids unnecessarily again. All I have is me and my behavior and my knowing that if I push hard to dig deep, to understand and accept my own role in The Orange Rhino Challenge, then I greatly increase my chances of not yelling.

Day 7: Revelations, Actions, and Tips

Orange Rhino Revelations

- It was easier to blame my kids' behavior for why I yelled instead of taking ownership that my personal challenges put me in an impatient place.

- **Nine times out of ten, my personal issues were the real triggers, not my sons' behavior.**

- What I learned about myself by "digging deep" not only helped me stop yelling but also helped me build more rewarding relationships with everyone in my life, not just my kids.

Today's Actions

- **Be honest with yourself.**

- **Keep tracking your triggers.** Make sure you are being honest with yourself about the real trigger. The goals of digging deep and getting uncomfortable are:

    ▸ To understand your role in the situation

    ▸ To gain awareness of the need to take ownership of your behavior

    ▸ To acknowledge any crap in your life that really brings you down

- **Use the "Why, mommy, why, why?" approach to dig deep.**

    ▸ It will be easy to write down surface-level answers such as, the kids left crayons out, the kids spilled milk, or the kids won't stop whining. Sometimes, surface-level triggers are the real triggers, and sometimes not. But if what you write down doesn't feel right, if your gut doesn't feel at ease, then start asking yourself, "Why am I really yelling?"

    ▸ You will know the truth when your gut goes, "Aha!" and when you don't question what you write down.

- **Use these questions to help you dig deep.**

    ▸ Are my kids really acting "bad" or am I just in a bad mood?

    ▸ Am I happy at this moment or sad, frustrated, stressed, anxious?

    ▸ Did I have a fight with someone lately?

    ▸ Is my to-do list overwhelming me today?

    ▸ Is one of these major (and rest assured, common) personal triggers pushing me to yell: work stress, marriage strife, weight, tiredness, lack of exercise, social problems, money problems, health challenges, lack of help, lack of faith in oneself as a parent (i.e., not really mad at child for not listening, mad at self for not knowing how to work with that child to listen)?

Tracking triggers and learning about yourself is going to be one of the biggest rewards of this challenge. So even when it feels annoying and like a waste of time, keep at it! The truth might be your child's behavior. Or it might be something going on in your life. Push yourself. It will be easier to lie, but it will be more helpful to be honest.

66 **If there is anything that we wish to** change in the child, we should first examine it and see whether it is not something that could better be changed in ourselves. **99**

—Carl Jung

Today's Tips

COOL 😐	Ask for a hug from your kids. Hugs from my kids throughout the day fill me with calm and help keep yelling attacks at bay. The more hugs throughout the day, the better!
WARM 😟	Ask your kids WHY they are crying. Chances are, there is a good reason, and you'll want to love your children instead of scream at them; besides, kids love to be listened to and given a chance to be understood.
HOT 😣	**Orange Rhino Favorite:** Turn a yell into gibberish to let off steam but still make people laugh instead of cry; my favorite word is "oogaschmoogabooga!"

Day 8

Note Physical Symptoms of a Growing Yell: Mommy Threw a Sippy Cup

Since I already admitted to you that I taught my kids to swear (unintentionally, remember?!), I feel a wee bit more comfortable confessing another embarrassing secret. Once (okay, probably twice), I felt so frustrated with my kids' not listening as we rushed out to school that I grabbed a sippy cup that I had just tripped over and threw it against the wall so hard that it made a dent. Of course, I also yelled at the same time, "GET IN THE CAR NOW OR ELSE!" As the sippy cup hit the door and my voice hit the "loud and scary level," milk sprayed every which way, including in my face. I snarfed in frustration, only to then snort milk up my nose. The boys all stopped and looked at me, scared as scared can be. Could I blame them? Nope.

I have never, ever shared this story with anyone until now.

I just carry such immense feelings of shame, embarrassment, and disappointment. I mean, really, how could I throw something in the direction of my kids that could hurt them, even if I made sure it wasn't directly at them? How could I be such a hypocrite to expect my kids to not throw blocks at each other's heads when mad, if I clearly demonstrated how to throw an even larger item toward a head? How could I not sense my frustration growing or that I was gonna blow? How could I be an adult and not control my anger? My impulses? My frustration? What was wrong with me?

Seriously, what was wrong with me? Well, for starters, I hadn't yet started The Orange Rhino Challenge, I had absolutely, positively no self-awareness whatsoever that being exhausted and feeling stretched thin would put me in such a bad place that a misplaced sippy cup would push me over the edge. And, I most definitely had no clue that my body actually had, and had most likely just sent off, several physical warning signals that I was about to lose my cool.

Nope, that fateful sippy-cup-throwing morning I didn't know that, if my hands are sweating and I didn't just work out, it most likely means I am getting wicked stressed, too stressed, and am about to lose it.

I didn't know that if my heart is racing and I didn't just finish playing Wii Dance with my kiddos, it probably means I am getting agitated, too agitated, and am about to lose it.

I didn't know that if my face starts to feel flushed and not because Channing Tatum just told me I was gorgeous (yeah, never happened, sigh), it means a yell is inching closer and closer and I am about to lose it.

Nope, it wasn't until The Orange Rhino Challenge that I figured out that my body had some pretty powerful S.O.S signals that it gives off to clue me in that I need to calm down. One night early on in the challenge, the exact day I do not recall, I as usual rounded up the boys for bath time. And as usual, within minutes of them splashing me, yelling at each other, and generally dilly-dallying, I felt a yell growing stronger and stronger. I then felt the all-too-familiar physical symptoms that I seemed to get every night at bath time: sweaty palms, a racing heart, and a flushed face. And then, instead of counting to ten to keep from letting out the usual and desired yell, I let out a big, "DUH!"

Duh, duh, duh!

You see, in my commitment to write down on sticky notes when I yelled and why, my mind had started becoming really good at naturally upping its "thinking and analyzing skills" around "yell time" so that it could gather any information that would help me change. That night at bath time, my brain had a breakthrough. Even though I don't remember the exact chitchat I had with myself, knowing me, it went like this.

"Dude, for the last two-plus years at bath time you have felt these same exact symptoms, the sweaty hands, the racing heart, the flushed face, and you have always yelled. Right now you feel these exact same feelings and you want to yell but can't and won't. Dude, these symptoms aren't because 'oh maybe this hot flash is just PMS' or 'maybe my hands are sweating because I didn't drink enough water today' like you always told yourself; they are your physical reaction to increased stress and the desire to yell!"

Yes, at just about every bath time for two years prior to The Orange Rhino Challenge, I felt all these symptoms and failed to make the connection between them and my big ole usual bath time yells of "Hurry up!" or "Don't splash me!" or "If you don't get your pajamas on now you are putting yourself to bed without snuggles or books." I don't know how I missed the connection; the symptoms were so intense that I can still quite clearly picture myself sitting on the bathroom floor, wiping my hands on my jeans and thinking, *"Oh my gosh, I am totally losing it and on top of it my heart is racing and I am wicked hot."* The yells were so intense that next to my "epiphany yell," bath time goes down as the next worst yelling moments (sadly, not just moment). Sigh.

Oh, how many moments my body tried to help me realize that I needed to calm down and I failed to realize it and just yelled away, setting myself, and my kids, up for a night not of feeling relaxed, but of feeling disappointed and ashamed. Oh, oh, how I would love to take back those bath-time memories and I would love, love, LOVE to take back the great-sippy-cup story that showed awesome parental immaturity.

But I can't.

I can, however, do as I have done ever since the "duh moment" in the bathroom. I can keep paying close attention to my physical signals of growing tension so that I don't repeat history and yell unnecessarily, or break any sippy cups or snarf milk. (Just saying, not doing those two things again is nice, too!)

Simple Alternates to Yelling

When my body signals me that a yell is seconds away, these are my top go-to alternatives to relieve some tension and get back to a happier place.

Left top: Keep the yell in; stick out your tongue and go "blahhhhhhh!"

Left center: Crunch an apple (or more!) a day to keep the yells away.

Left bottom: Squeeze, don't scream!

Right top: Force a smile, force the yell away!

Right center: Close your eyes and picture a beach; allow the wave of negative emotion to pass.

Right bottom: Block out the noise, block out the desire to yell!

Day 8: Revelations, Actions, and Tips

Orange Rhino Revelations

- **My body gives me pretty obvious warning signs (besides a louder and louder voice) that I am going to lose it.**
- Learning those physical symptoms and paying attention to them is an awesome way to prevent yelling.

Today's Actions

- **Note physical symptoms of growing yells.**
- **Continue tracking triggers** so you can keep gaining insights as to what areas you need to focus on.
  - ▸ Learn from what you write down. If you write down, "I yelled because we were late," then push yourself to understand why you were late. Were you disorganized? Overslept? Lost track of time?
- **Start paying attention to how you physically feel before and during a yell.**
- **Record physical symptoms of oncoming yells** on the tracking sheet and/or below. This information will help you recognize when a yell is coming.
  - ▸ Are your hands sweaty? Are you fidgety, especially with your hands? Is your heart racing? Do you suddenly feel really hot? Do you feel like you could punch a wall? Do you want to pull your hair out?

_____

_____

_____

_____

_____

_____

_____

_____

_____

_____

I know that tracking triggers and seeing all this new data about yourself can be uncomfortable, scary, and sad at times. Please trust me that it is actually a good thing for you, because it will help you change and yell less.

66 **I think self-awareness is probably the most** important thing towards being a champion. **99**

—Billie Jean King

Today's Tips

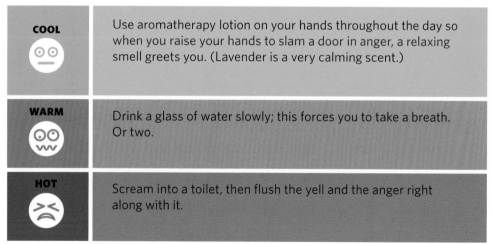

COOL	Use aromatherapy lotion on your hands throughout the day so when you raise your hands to slam a door in anger, a relaxing smell greets you. (Lavender is a very calming scent.)
WARM	Drink a glass of water slowly; this forces you to take a breath. Or two.
HOT	Scream into a toilet, then flush the yell and the anger right along with it.

Day 9

Label Your Triggers: "No, I Won't Clean My Room!"

Edward loves, loves, loves to clean his room. In fact, he loves it so much that he never, ever, EVER drops to the floor in a heap of tears and pounds his fists into the carpet while screaming, "I hate cleaning my room" and "No, I won't clean my room!" Nope, instead he runs to me every morning and says, "Oh Mommy, I just can't wait to clean my room!" Oh, oh how I wish this were true; it sure would make my mornings so much calmer!

But it isn't. Every single morning Edward and I have the distinct pleasure of engaging in a discussion about how he needs to pick up all the toys, stuffed animals, and books that he took out while playing in his room when the rest of the house was asleep. And every single morning Edward insists that he just "can't clean his room."

One day during said battle, as I stood with Captain Hook and his pirate friends attacking one foot, and as I desperately fought off the part of me that wanted to yell. **I decided to recall one of the many lessons The Orange Rhino Challenge taught me. I decided to actually stop discussing and demanding and start listening and asking. Maybe there was a legitimate reason to all these tantrums.** Maybe not, but maybe. I wouldn't know if I didn't actually give my son a chance to express his thoughts on the matter.

"Okay, Edward, tell me, why can't you clean your room?"

"Because there is too much of a mess," he replied.

I of course wanted to respond with, *"Well, duh. You haven't listened to me when I try to teach you to put things away as you go so that you don't have a big mess in the end."* I of course knew that this would not be the most empathetic or helpful response, so I bit my tongue and went along.

"There is a huge mess, you are right. But you can do it, I know you can."

"But Mommy, I just don't know where to start. It's too much," he said sobbing.

"Okay, what if we work together?"

"But Mommy, I told you already, it is too much. We will never get it done."

"Yes, we will, come on."

"Mommmmmmyyyyy, I told you it's TOO MUCH!" he cried, this time near hysterics.

"Yes, I know you mentioned that," I thought bitterly. Eeerck. STOP. He was telling me the exact reason he couldn't clean his room; I just wasn't totally listening. It was too much—he was too overwhelmed. And I got it. So, I tried again.

"Okay, Edward. I get it. You are right. It does feel like there is too much. Let's go bit by bit together, okay? We don't have to do it all at once; we can do one part at a time. 'Kay? Trust me."

And so we cleaned up his room bit by bit. First we put the pirates away, then the Legos, then the Smurfs, then the books, then the drawer full of socks, and finally, we made his bed.

"All done! See, we did it, Edward! We took one thing at a time and it was easy, right?" I said enthusiastically, thrilled that I had kept my calm.

"Yes, Mommy, thank you," he said sweetly as he came over and gave me a hug. You know, I might not love his morning mess, but I do love his morning hugs and how grateful my little bugger can be.

Edward proceeded to get dressed and I proceeded to thank The Orange Rhino Challenge for drilling the "bit by bit, one moment at a time" mentality into my head. Prior to the challenge, that was just *not* a mentality I embraced when overwhelmed. Instead, like Edward, I froze when everything felt like too much. I panicked. I did the exact opposite of what I needed to get done, and so I did … nothing. Doing nothing, of course, made my feelings of being overwhelmed even greater, so I would keep doing nothing, and my feelings would keep growing and growing until I chose to do something. That something? Calling my husband or my own mommy, crying that I just "can't do it," just like Edward sobbed to me that morning, and every morning. And if I couldn't reach my husband or mom, and I still felt overwhelmed? Well, then, I would yell unneccessarily at my kids.

Of course, I didn't realize this yucky connection between feeling overwhelmed and yelling until I started tracking triggers and realized that one of my biggest "it's not you, it's me" triggers was indeed being overwhelmed. Yep, it was enlightening, motivating, and helpful to be gaining a deeper understanding of why I yelled, BUT at first, it was also overwhelming. All the information gave me a solid plan … but a plan with lots of steps. So much to work on! So much so that I am fairly certain I called hubby and my mom at least once a week crying that "I just can't do it."

> My hubby always said, "Yes you can. What is that quotation you love by Herb Kelleher (cofounder of Southwest Airlines)? 'Think small and act small, and we'll get bigger. Think big and act big, and we'll get smaller.' So think small; think one thing at a time."

My hubby always said, "Yes you can. What is that quotation you love by Herb Kelleher (cofounder of Southwest Airlines)? 'Think small and act small, and we'll get bigger. Think big and act big, and we'll get smaller.' So think small; think one thing at a time."

My mom always said, "Just go one moment at a time. Focus on one trigger, one goal at a time. You can do it."

They were both right. I forced myself to take a step back and look at all my triggers and find the smallish, easier ones to focus on first. It turned out that there were lots of easy ones to fix, that all my triggers weren't big, gigantic, overwhelming ones. I then took one trigger at a time, one small step at a time. And I reminded myself every time I got overwhelmed with either the challenge or any other big pressing issue to "think small;

go bit by bit, moment by moment." Before I knew it, I had alleviated many of the small triggers and felt less and less overwhelmed by the daunting task of not yelling. Were there times, are there still times, when I want to cry and pound my fists into the ground like Edward because everything feels like too much? Yes. HECK, YEAH. But at least now I know how to manage it so that I don't freeze and, more importantly, so I don't yell!

66 Don't be afraid to give your best
to what seemingly are small jobs.
Every time you conquer one,
it makes you that much stronger.
If you do the little jobs well,
the big ones will tend to take care
of themselves. **99**

—Dale Carnegie

Day 9: Revelations, Actions, and Tips

Orange Rhino Revelations

- All my triggers didn't actually carry the same weight of difficulty to overcome.

- Identifying and focusing on the easier triggers first gave me quick wins and boosted my confidence so that I could tackle the larger ones—one trigger at a time.

- Some of my triggers overwhelmed me because I knew they couldn't be changed or controlled by me, but just knowing this and labeling them as such made them less overwhelming and easier to handle.

Today's Actions

- **Track your triggers for the last "official" day.** If you think a few more days would be good, then go for it. There is no limit! Just remember after a bit to come back here and follow the rest of the day's suggested actions so that you can turn the trigger data into how-to-yell-less data.

- **Label your triggers at the end of the day.** Review all four days of trigger tracking and group triggers into: Fixable Triggers, Manageable Triggers, and Unchangeable Triggers.

  - ▸ **Fixable Triggers:** Think of these as the easy ones, the quick wins where an easy solution exists to remove the trigger completely. Examples: morning rush (pack bags night before), noise (wear earmuffs or create quiet zones in the house), kids forgetting morning routine (post picture schedule in bedroom).

  - ▸ **Manageable Triggers:** These triggers aren't always present but you can learn to prepare for them so that when they do pop up, you can manage your response. In some cases, with enough practice, they might even become close to extinct as a trigger. Examples: fight with spouse, PMS, children fighting, being tired.

  - ▸ **Unchangeable Triggers:** These are the triggers that are out of your control because you can't remove them from your life, either at all or under the timetable you wish. They probably challenge you daily. Examples: health issues, past traumatic events, other people's behavior. They don't need to be huge: They might even be as simple as "husband won't make bed."

Don't worry about labeling your triggers correctly; just focus on grouping them because this will help you break down the task of yelling less into smaller steps.

66 **The secret of getting ahead is getting started.**
The secret of getting started is breaking your complex, overwhelming tasks into small manageable tasks, and starting on the first one. **99**

—Mark Twain

Today's Tips

COOL	**Orange Rhino Favorite:** Close your eyes and picture yourself on a beach, perhaps with a fancy drink with an umbrella in hand. This takes you to a happy, peaceful place. To make the trip even better, let your kids know you are going. When I say, "Mommy is going to Machu Picchu," my kids know I need a "me" break!
	Make a did-do list of all you have done today, and include loving and hugging your kids. This keeps you from getting overwhelmed by the other to-do list and focuses your attention on what matters most.
WARM	Laugh, even if you don't want to! Laughter is good for the soul and can bring great perspective.
HOT	Plan a scream with the kids. When the tension is too high and a scream is inevitable, invite the kiddos to run outside and scream with you.

Practice Trigger Management

> **The most difficult thing is the decision** to act, the rest is merely tenacity. You can do anything you decide to do. You can act to change and control your life; and the procedure, the process is its own reward.
>
> —Amelia Earhart

I have fairly vivid memories from my childhood of my mom telling me that I needed to practice piano if I wanted to play better and my dad telling me that practicing my math problems would make them easier ... and I remember hating it when they both told me to practice! So, if you hate me right now for using the word *practice*, I get it. I mean really, who likes to practice? *Not me!* When I started The Orange Rhino Challenge, I just wanted to wake up and be a nonyelling parent; I didn't want to have to practice! But, I needed to. It took me four tries and about two weeks of practicing until I had enough awareness of how to spot an oncoming yell, of which alternatives work best for which triggers, and which alternatives don't work, to be able to then go forward successfully toward my goal. I know you probably want to jump in already and officially go after your personal goal of not yelling (we'll get there, I promise), but trust me, the process of practicing these next five days will give you a reward you don't want to miss.

Day 10

Fix the Fixable Triggers:
Clutter Makes Me Want to Scream

So, not only do I often have a little "Orange Rhino" in my head warning me when I am about to lose it, but I also sometimes have the little yellow birdie from P.D. Eastman's *Big Dog, Little Dog* in my head. She sits right next to The Orange Rhino and when necessary, reminds me how to handle life. The birdie has been around since one night when I finished reading the last part of her book, which goes:

    The next morning, Fred said, "My bed is too little!"

"My bed is too big!" said Ted.

"I know what to do!" said the bird.

"Ted should sleep upstairs and Fred should sleep downstairs!"

... Ted slept all day long in the cozy little bed. And Fred slept all day long in the cozy big bed.

"Well, that was easy to do. Big dogs need big beds. Little dogs need little beds.

Why make big problems out of little problems?"

Seriously. Why make big problems out of little problems? I mean, really, why? Problems are hard enough as it is, so why make them bigger? Or put another way, why take a little yelling trigger and escalate it by actually yelling ridiculously? I learned early on that all yelling does is make my boys cry, which then makes a once little trigger feel ginormous because now I have a sad, upset child on hand to deal with as well as whatever set me off initially. So it's totally not worth taking something small and blowing it out of proportion.

> I learned early on that all yelling does is make my boys cry, which then makes a once little trigger feel ginormous because now I have a sad, upset child on hand to deal with as well as whatever set me off initially.

Which is why when I read that line "Why make big problems out of little problems?" I laughed. A little bird (okay, P.D. Eastman, but work with me) summarized so simply what I had struggled with earlier that day. I took a very small problem, like an infinitesimally small problem, and almost yelled over it. Really?!

You see, I had gotten into a total hissy fit over sorting the laundry. Yes, you read that correctly: hissy fit over laundry. I threw a mini temper tantrum because, as usual, I couldn't match all the socks! Can you please tell me why the size of the sock is printed in the same color as the sock, so that I have to strain my eyes to read it? I mean, come on, the size is on the bottom of the foot! No one will see it, who cares what color the print is?! I just want to be able to read it so I can get my kids' socks matched and I can get on with my day!

Okay, rant over. Moving on. Anywho, so I was annoyed and my boys dared to ask me questions while Mac tried to "help" me with the laundry (by emptying the laundry basket). This was clearly an "It's not you, it's me" moment, by the way, but still, ARGHH! I started to get all snappy and I could feel my desire to yell growing. Luckily, the phone rang and my yell, and the laundry, got pushed aside. Silly problem not solved, just not blown up into a yell.

That night as I read to Andrew and the little yellow bird said to me, *"Why make big problems out of little problems?"* it hit me. I did have a simple solution to the sock problem. I started to do some basic math.

4 kids + 2 parents = 6 people.

The week = 7 days.

That means instead of mixing all the laundry and having to sort it at night I could do one person's laundry each day and never have to sort and match socks again—such a simple, easy solution, really. When I say this solution changed my life, that is an understatement. Okay, it's an overstatement, but it is pretty gosh darn close! I no longer had to sort clothes or match socks; this saved me a good twenty minutes of time and frustration a day! Such a simple solution, truly. (Did I mention that?)

Why hadn't I thought of this laundry solution earlier? It certainly wasn't for a lack of laundry; there was plenty of it! Nope, it was because I hadn't stopped and thought about how to solve the problem, which is kind of ironic because that is exactly what I had been doing for the last eleven straight months thanks to The Orange Rhino Challenge. You see, as soon as I started tracking my triggers, I saw that I had so many easy-to-solve triggers. All I had to do was stop, brainstorm solutions, and *poof*, trigger be gone.

Trigger: Getting all agitated right before dinnertime because I didn't know what to cook or what meal I could even cook given the food in the house … and the boys are all chomping at the bit, making it impossible to think.

Simple Solution: Make a menu for the week every Saturday morning, grocery shop for said menu, write said menu down by fridge, and voilà! No stress over what to cook and no worry over not having ingredients!

Trigger: James dumps all his LEGOs on the floor so he can sort through them easier, making it (1) impossible to walk into his room without injuring my feet and (2) impossible to get him to clean them up because it takes FOREVER.

Simple Solution: Bought a large under the bed sweater bin and dumped all the LEGOs in; now he pulls it out and doesn't have to dump because he can sort right in it. Score!

Trigger: The morning rush. Um, enough said? Between finding backpacks and shoes, going to the bathroom, getting jackets, and getting in the car, my easily distracted kiddos take so long that I want to scream "marching orders" to move them along.

Simple Solution: Take backpacks and lunch bags out the night before and place in the kitchen for quick access in the morning. It's only one less thing, but every "one less thing" matters.

And one of my biggest yet smallest triggers … **CLUTTER!**

Trigger: Oh clutter, oh clutter, how I loathe you!

I still vividly remember walking into the kitchen one morning not too long before The Orange Rhino Challenge and seeing piles of sh*t all over the kitchen and the family room. Everywhere my eyes turned loose papers taunted me, primary-colored toys taunted me, shoes taunted me. They all said, "Neener, neener, neener, we're out of place, don't you hate it?!" Um, Yes! Andrew then innocently and ever so sweetly said "Mommy?" and I roared, I mean ROARED back at him, "What do you want?!" Understandably, he burst into tears.

"I just wanted to say good morning and give you hug."

Well, who was the pile of sh*t now?

Moi.

I looked at my husband, tears in my eyes. "Honey. Everywhere I turn is sh*t to be put away. It is never ending. I know I am supposed to let it go, but I can't. It reminds me of ALL I have to do and yet never get to. It reminds me of how chaotic my day is, how I am never caught up. It drives me nuts!"

"It's okay," he reassured me, but really, it wasn't. I wanted to scream some more. I wanted to grab garbage bags and fill them with all the piles of paper and out of place toys and then head to the dump.

But what I really wanted that morning, and EVERY MORNING, was not just a clean counter, but some order. Clean counters bring me calm. Clean closets bring me calm. Clean bedrooms bring me calm. Because they represent order. And right now with four young kids, I hardly have real order and I crave it. It keeps me grounded. It keeps me sane. And my simple solution that I finally discovered now keeps me sane ... and yelling less!

Simple Solution: Every night, no matter what, I take five minutes, sometimes ten if I have it, and put away any and all clutter I see. This simple solution is right up there with my laundry solution for changing my life. How do I know? Because since I stopped and thought of a solution to this yelling trigger, every morning I now come down to a clean counter and I can breathe and keep my cool even when the four kids are all asking for juice, milk, water, fruit, and cereal at once. How else do I know? Well, on the days when I do not take this short time, it takes me a lot longer to get to a calm place where I don't want to yell.

Oh, there are so many triggers to yell in my life, and it takes time to identify them. But the good news? So many of them are easily solved if I just take a moment to think. The other good news? Just thinking for a bit about these small problems has kept them from creating big problems, that is children with hurt feelings and a mama filled with remorse and guilt. I'd say it is worth the time and effort, wouldn't you?

Orange Rhino Revelations

- Yelling makes things worse. No matter how big or small the original trigger, yelling will most definitely exacerbate the original issue.

- Yelling doesn't solve anything. Stopping, thinking, and planning can, however, solve things.

Today's Actions

- **Fix the fixable triggers.** Copy all the triggers you labeled as fixable onto a new piece of paper. Label that list: Quick Orange Rhino Wins.

- **Identify one to work on solving today and solve it.** Take five to ten minutes to think about the problem and brainstorm solutions. If relevant, ask your kids if they have ideas for solutions as well. Including them will make it easier to execute.

- **Put a check next to the trigger when you have succeeded in removing it so you feel proud.** Seriously! If you find you have leftover time and energy, pick another on the list. Check it off when done.

- **Keep your "Quick Orange Rhino Wins" list posted in an area you hang out in a lot.** On future days when you feel down about your success, review the list and see all you have achieved. And then pick an "easy win" and achieve that to increase your confidence.

❝ Think left and think right and think low and think high. Oh, the thinks you can think up if only you try! ❞

—Dr. Seuss

Today's Tips

COOL ☺☺	Place orange flowers in a vase in the kitchen. The smallest things (flowers) can bring you the biggest pleasure; when you feel happy, you yell less.
WARM ☺☺	Get the camera. Taking a picture of small annoyances forces you to see behavior that probably doesn't deserve a big-time yell; it also serves as a great source of laughter.
	Walk away. You can't solve a problem by yelling. Walking away literally keeps you from yelling but also gives you the opportunity to think, gain perspective, and problem solve. (So simple and yet so hard to do, I know!)
HOT 😣	Start drumming the table/counter until rage is gone. This is a really good stress reliever and can start a dance party, which helps everyone chill out.

Capture the moment, capture the desire to yell! (I, of course, always make sure my munchkins are safe before getting the camera!)

Day 11

Manage the Manageable Triggers:
My S.P.D. Makes Me Y.E.L.L.

I am going to let you in on a very personal struggle, one that I have only shared with a handful of people in my life because it is so embarrassing and frustrating that I have just hid it and ignored it for years. Oh, how I hoped that it would just magically disappear and that I would finally be free of the pain and shame I feel whenever it rears its wicked ugly head (which, by the way, is at least three or four times a day). But it never disappeared and once I started The Orange Rhino Challenge, I could no longer hide from it, or run from it. When I started tracking my triggers and gaining deeper awareness as to what made me explode, I discovered—or rather, was finally forced to admit—that this little struggle of mine wasn't just real, but it was also a really big (like gargantuan) trigger. Yes, there was no ignoring the fact that if I wanted to stop yelling, I needed to start managing this struggle of mine STAT no matter how hard it was.

Ya' ready for my struggle?

I have Sensory Processing Disorder, also known as S.P.D.

Um, what the heck does that mean, you ask?

It means that I have "sensory attacks," brought on by any, or all, of my five senses being overloaded to the point where I can't keep myself together and I go from calm(ish) to anything-but in a split second. It might come on from too much noise or too much chaos, or maybe I feel too hot or my clothes feel too tight or itchy, or maybe I taste a mushy food or smell a disgusting odor, or maybe it is a combination of all of the above that sends my body "under attack." Sometimes the attacks come completely out of the blue; sometimes I sense they are coming. It can take thirty minutes to an entire day to feel calm again and in control of my body after an attack (and it takes a lot longer to forget the embarrassment and disgrace I feel for losing it).

During a "sensory attack," I literally feel the physical desire to lose it in a rather aggressive manner. I feel like the inside of my body is on fire, that my body is trying to burn my skin so that it can get out and escape. I feel like I want to run away at full speed and keep running until I cool down, until my heart stops beating so hard my chest hurts, until my skin stops itching so much that I want to tear it off, until the intensity that overwhelmed me stops. My body, my mind, and my soul want to flee the intense physical response and displeasure they feel from the sensory attack, but they can't.

I feel trapped and that's because I am trapped, trapped at the mercy of the "sensory attack," and all I can do once an attack has hit is to wait it out. And since I can't flee the pain or the frustration, I fight. I fight my body by throwing things. I fight my body by crying. I have even fought my body by pulling my hair, by hitting my head. **And I used to fight by yelling.**

I would love to write that my children have never witnessed one of my attacks, that they never saw me shove my dinner plate across the table and then refuse to eat because my Italian sausage was just the wrong texture at the wrong time. I would love to write that my boys never saw me tear a brand-new (and very fashionable and cool!) scarf off from around my neck and throw it in the garbage while yelling, "I hate clothes. Hate them, hate them, hate them! Nothing ever feels right!" I would love to write that they never watched me go berserk when my husband turned on a sports radio show to catch "the big game" and all the scratchy noise of the poor reception made me start screaming at him uncontrollably to turn it off before I exploded. Yeah, I would love to say they have never witnessed any of the above, but that would be a lie.

And I would love, even more so, to write that my children were never the targets of one of my sensory attacks, but that would also be a lie. The bad news is that they have indeed been on the receiving end of one of my sensory moments, but the good news (okay, better than bad news) is that at least it was yelling and not worse. Oh, oh, how I have screamed at them when my body just couldn't handle another noise, no matter how discreet or unintentional.

> In finally having a more complete awareness of the depth of the problem, I was able to start actually managing it to the point where it is no longer as major an issue, which let me tell you, is nothing short of awesome.

I have yelled, "Back up now, or else!" when my kids innocently chewed popcorn near me, not next to me, but just near me, and with their mouths open so that I could hear every crunch.

I have yelled, "Be quiet NOW, it is just too much! I can't stand it. I am going to leave!" when all my boys are talking at once and getting louder and louder so that they can each be heard over each other.

I have yelled, "Okay, enough of the hugging! I don't want to be touched anymore! Get off of me!" Yeah, that was an awful thing to say, and worse, I have said it a lot.

And I have yelled at myself after the fact, *"Get a grip! If all you want is for your kids to be quiet and not overly playful because you can't handle noise and chaos, then why did you have kids?! And four of them?! All you do is constantly squash their joy and enthusiasm just because mommy can't handle it. Seriously?"* I have tried so hard my entire life to keep my S.P.D. under control and hidden. And when I became a mom, I did learn to control it better because there is nothing I wanted more than to love my kids and not unleash my wrath on them. And I did keep it under control many moments. But yes, there were moments that I didn't, and those left me beyond humiliated, beyond discouraged, beyond heartbroken.

But the good news, yes, the really good news, is that The Orange Rhino Challenge forced me to finally manage my S.P.D. **My S.P.D. no longer causes me to Y.E.L.L.—Yell Exceptionally Long and Loud—because tracking my triggers increased my awareness and forced me to figure out how to manage this really big trigger.** And luckily for me, at the same time that I became aware of and accepted my S.P.D. as a trigger, one of my sons started some occupational therapy for his own struggles with S.P.D.

Everything he learned, everything he told me, and every exercise we did together to "help him" actually helped me learn how to manage my own S.P.D.

I learned to do push-ups when I felt an attack coming on.

I learned to put earmuffs on when the noise overwhelmed me.

I learned to pull my fingers gently to calm down.

I learned to eat crunchy foods like apples to organize my mind when it felt fried.

I learned to take deep breaths, even though I hated to, big-time.

I learned to prioritize sleep because it is key to regulating my mood.

In fact, all these little tricks worked so well to help me cool down and prevent and put out sensory attacks that I decided to try them to help me cool down and prevent and put out yelling attacks as well. Well, wouldn't you know ... my S.P.D. tricks work great on Y.E.L.L. attacks too!

Looking back, learning to manage my S.P.D. has been a heck of a lot easier than I expected. Have I been able to make it completely disappear, as I have dreamed of for years? No, I am just The Orange Rhino, not a fairy godmother! But, in finally having a more complete awareness of the depth of the problem, I was able to start actually managing it to the point where it is no longer as major an issue, which let me tell you, is nothing short of awesome. Not only am I now much more able to model how to control emotions and calm down, but I am also not yelling at my kids unnecessarily. Take these two pieces together and I feel like a much better person and parent. (A person and parent who, by the way, is crying right now because she feels so much gratitude that she started her journey to stop yelling and that it helped her overcome such a large personal struggle she has been fighting for years.)

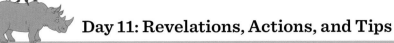

Orange Rhino Revelations

- Ignoring a trigger because I assume that there is no way to manage it does me no good; acknowledging a trigger and trying to understand it and manage it does me a lot of good.

- Gaining more control of a trigger than I thought possible is invigorating, but I never would have learned that if I kept running from the trigger because it intimidated me.

Today's Actions

- **Manage the manageable triggers.** Pick one trigger that you labeled as "manageable" to work on today. Brainstorm ways you can limit the trigger and how you can respond to it when it occurs. Perhaps involve friends or family in the brainstorm; more heads can be better than one.

- **Write down the trigger with your goals of how to manage it so it feels real and keeps you on track.** Example:

  ▸ Trigger: Kids refusing to eat dinner.

  ▸ Plan: Offer at least one food each child likes as part of meal. Tacos for child 1, black beans for child 2, corn for all.

  ▸ Alternative to yelling if plan doesn't work: Use orange napkins at mealtime as reminder to stay calm.

As you tackle this trigger, remember that you are practicing and that it takes time to learn how to yell less. Struggling is part of the process. As Frederick Douglass said, *"If there is no struggle, there is no progress."* You are making progress; learning how to manage a trigger is indeed progress. Don't fret if you don't master it today—there are several more days of practicing ahead!

❝ Acceptance doesn't mean resignation; it means understanding that something is what it is and that there's got to be a way through it. ❞

—Michael J. Fox

Today's Tips

COOL	Wear earmuffs or noise-canceling headphones during known loud times to prevent noise overload (can we say the first few minutes after trick-or-treating in candy-induced craziness?).
	Say "thank you." The more outwardly grateful I am, the happier I am. And the happier I am, the more love I feel. And, well, the more love I feel, the less I want to yell.
WARM	Chew gum. Chomping out my frustration keeps me from spitting out mean words!
HOT	Grab Play-Doh (or Silly Putty, or a kitchen towel, or anything safe) and squeeze, but don't scream; keep squeezing until there is no energy left to scream.

Day 12

Acknowledge the Unchangeable Triggers: The Twenty-Five-Hour Day

The Christmas after James was born, I asked Santa Claus to bring me one extra hour in the day. I don't think he received my letter because I didn't get that extra hour. Or maybe he did receive the letter, but ignored my request because he didn't like the fact that I put out two homemade cookies instead of three. Or maybe, and this is a big maybe, he chose to give me a new scarf and jacket instead of the extra hour because, despite all the magical things he can do, making the day have twenty-five hours instead of twenty-four is just not one of them, no matter how good a girl I was that year.

Sigh. I don't think I am ever getting that twenty-fifth hour from Santa Claus. Or from anyone, for that matter.

All the hoping and wishing in the world can't give me that so desperately desired twenty-fifth hour. Nothing can change the fact that the day has twenty-four hours and always will. I know this. I mean, I am a somewhat smart girl, and I get it. And yet, I don't get it. Because if I really got it, if I really, really accepted the fact that the day will never have twenty-five hours, then I wouldn't try to do as many things as I do because I would know that I physically can't do it all with the amount of time I have.

Actually, let me rephrase. Can I do everything that I try to do? Can I manage the demands of four kids' therapy schedules, extracurricular activities, and personal needs and wants, all while also tending to my marriage and working to keep the flame alive during the difficult years of raising young children? And can I do all of that while also keeping in touch with my friends as much as I want and need and they deserve? And can I do all of that while also volunteering at three different schools because I feel as a mom that I need to be there to support my boys? Oh and wait, can I do all of that while also managing the house, and trying to manage my mood by making sure that I do some things for me that nourish my soul, such as exercise, writing, and going out of my way to do random acts of kindness for friends, family, and strangers?

Theoretically, yeah, I can.

I can do all of it.

I can stay up late every night and wake up early every morning so that I can do everything that I *want* to do. I can push and push myself to the extremes to squeeze everything into twenty-four hours a day because I want to do it all. And then when that is all done, I can cry to my husband that I yelled at the kids again because I am so tired. I can cry to my mom that I yelled at the kids again because I feel so disappointed in myself that I am not doing anything to the quality that I wish, that I am not enjoying anything because I am always worrying about what else I have to do. I can cry to myself that I yelled at the kids again because I am so overwhelmed and stressed that every little move pushes my buttons.

So yeah, I can do it all in twenty-four hours a day.

But I pay a price.

And so do my children (and probably everyone in my life, for that matter). Trying to do too much in the time I have, not taking *"no, you can't do it; you don't have the time"* for an answer—shoot, not giving "no" as an answer—is one of my biggest triggers for yelling. In fact, of all my triggers that I have tackled since I began my challenge, I am bold enough to say that this is the one trigger that I haven't been able to really get under control.

The truth is, I like to say yes and try to do it all. I like to push myself to achieve all that I can. I like to try to do as much as I can in my children's lives to make them feel special, such as decorating for each holiday, writing them little love notes, hosting creative birthday parties. And I like trying to do nice surprises for my friends and husband, not just because it gives me joy and hopefully them too, but also because I like showing my kids how to do nice things for others. And I like seizing opportunities; I am really good at telling myself, *"Oh, I just have to do this now. There will never be another chance. This. Is. It. You can do it. GO."*

> ... not taking *"no, you can't do it; you don't have the time"* for an answer—shoot, not giving "no" as an answer—is one of my biggest triggers for yelling.

The other truth, though, the more important truth, is that I often don't like the result: being moody because of my "push yourself to the limit" personality. I don't like snapping at my kids more because of my mood. I don't like yelling at them because I tried to do too much.

I distinctly remember one day during The Challenge when I was trying to get my no-yelling streak going again. I had taken on too much. I had just told myself to stop yelling, which, as you know, is a huge commitment. I was also trying to lose weight. The holidays had ended, so I figured, hey, perfect time to add some new projects to the plate. My plate overflowed and my shortness, impatience, and frustration at myself for wanting and trying to do too much overflowed as well.

While I looked at my to-do list and started trying to figure out how I would get everything done, my boys all happily played together in the playroom. They had peacefully and joyfully taken out all the different types of blocks, all the cars, and all the people, had taken down all the pillows from the couches, and had created a big city/fort/I don't know what it was. What did I think it was, though? A mess. I looked up from my list, lost in my own self-induced overwhelmed world, and yelled.

"Look at this mess! This is just awful! It's going to take forever to clean up!" I roared.

Eight eyes looked at me in despair that I had just declared their beautiful creation a mess, that I had just criticized and totally dismissed their working together, playing together, building together. It was so unnecessary.

It wasn't a mess. I was a mess.

Sadness overwhelmed me. This wasn't the first time I had yelled over something that was really nothing. I used to yell over truly trivial things. Like slurping Popsicles. I mean, really, slurping Popsicles deserves being yelled at? That is just ridiculous. It hit me at that moment that I often yelled at my sons when they were just enjoying life (and doing so in an appropriate manner, for that matter) and that every time I yelled at them in such situations, **my yells often squashed their love for life and took their joy and smiles away.**

That realization at that moment kicked me in the ass.

But yelling wasn't the only thing that needed to stop. I needed to stop thinking that the day has twenty-five hours and that I can do everything I want to do. I needed—no, wanted—to start embracing life more like my boys instead of bracing for the negative impact of trying to do too much.

That day I added the trigger "thinking that I can do everything" to the list. Although I have fully acknowledged that there will never be twenty-five hours in a day, that I simply can't do everything, and that I will never be able to be everything to everyone at once, I can't say I have fully accepted it. Because while I am doing better at not taking on as much, and embracing the notion that loving my kids, friends, and family doesn't have to mean doing *everything* for them, I still find myself filling my plate to the brim, thinking that suddenly these facts will magically change.

But they won't.

I need to fully acknowledge that these facts won't change if I want this trigger to stop being such an issue for me. Because once I do, then I will more readily stop causing my days to overflow with unneccessary stress. Instead, I want my days to overflow with loving experiences with my boys.

Day 12: Revelations, Actions, and Tips

Orange Rhino Revelations

- Acknowledging triggers that I cannot change is at first maddening, but then it is freeing because I no longer have to spend energy trying to change them and my attitude—I just have to focus on changing my attitude.

- Kids are indeed just kids and do just kid things, and I cannot change that no matter how hard I try, and definitely no matter how much I yell.

Today's Actions

- **Acknowledge the unchangeable triggers.** Review your triggers and identify one unchangeable trigger to focus on.

- **Write down notes as to why the trigger won't change.** Then write down notes as to the many benefits of you changing your attitude around this trigger. Example: Husband won't start making the bed because he hasn't for ten years. But, if I acknowledge that, stop nagging, and do it myself, I will start the day happier.

- **Share your notes with your support network to fully embrace that the trigger won't change.** The more you share, the more natural it will become to acknowledge that the trigger won't change, but that you can.

I know that today's revelations and actions are hard to read and even harder to embrace. Be gentle on yourself today as you process these thoughts, and know that having to think about difficult subjects such as unchangeable triggers can be a trigger in itself! Surround yourself with reminders of your promise, friends who are cheering you on, and the knowledge that this difficult day will lead to many an easier day in the future!

❝ There are two things a person should never be angry at, what they can help, and what they cannot. ❞

—Plato

Today's Tips

COOL	Turn the lights off; this stops kids in their tracks (huh, what happened?) and instantly calms things down. For a bonus effect at dinnertime, light a candle and have a candlelit meal.
WARM	Call a family meeting in the middle of the chaos; invite each child to discuss the problem and share solutions.
HOT	Say the child's age out loud; this forces you to remember that your child is just a kid. "Oh my gosh, you are just four!" Right, four years old. Not forty. Of course he is still learning to listen!

❝ Great things are not done by impulse,
but by a series of small things brought together. ❞

—Vincent Van Gogh

Day 13

Accept the Unchangeable Triggers:
I Can't Change My Son

Andrew had had fevers before, but right after his first birthday, he had the first one of "those" fevers. Those fevers meaning a fever that hit anywhere between 104°F and 105°F (40°C and 40.5°C) and lasted for a week to ten days. Those fevers meaning that with the fever his mouth and throat got so sore that he could barely eat or drink, but would cry and scream because the pain was too much. Those fevers meaning that when the fever broke, he was so hungry and tired from the long week prior, that he would also cry and scream for another week because he didn't have the words to tell us what he wanted. Those fevers that ended up being diagnosed and referred to as Periodic Fever Syndrome.

As his mom, though, as the one living with him day in and day out during his episodes, I gave them a different diagnosis. My official diagnosis? Fevers that taught him to scream bloody hell. Fevers that delayed his learning to speak. Fevers that made him miserable. Fevers that made me miserable. Fevers that made me yell—really, really yell.

And as I write that, tears are hitting the keyboard. My baby, my sweet Andrew, suffered so much for the ten long months that he had these monthly fevers. So much of his second year of life he spent uncomfortable, and there was nothing I could do about it. Nothing. His screaming from pain and from frustration that he couldn't yet tell us what he wanted or needed drove me to scream. There were days when I just couldn't handle it and I screamed right back at him, "STOP!" or "ENOUGH!" I was mean. I was hurtful. I wasn't understanding. Such days were few and far between, but still, I just wasn't loving in those moments, not even close.

I was just angry.

I wasn't angry at him, of course; I was angry at the situation. I was angry that we just had to wait and see if he had the type of Periodic Fever Syndrome that he would outgrow by age ten, or if he would have it for life. I was angry that I couldn't help him, that I couldn't change his problem and make it go away. I was angry that anytime we went out in public, I feared that one of his screaming fits would hit because in being sick most of each month, screaming and crying had become more his norm and therefore, sadly enough, it was often his default for communicating, sick or not.

And I was angry because I hadn't accepted our new norm. I didn't want to accept that this might be a long-term thing. I didn't want to accept the screaming fits. I didn't want to accept that sometimes all the best parenting tips in the world couldn't stop said fits. I didn't want to accept that going out in public meant facing judgment and criticism of myself as a parent, and my son as a kid. I didn't want to accept that what was probably a small speech delay to start was exacerbated by the fevers, meaning that we not only struggled to understand his needs when he was sick, but we also struggled to understand him when he was not sick. And I didn't want to accept that my hearing the words "Mommy, I love you" were so far off.

Nope, I didn't want to accept any part of the situation. So I harbored my feelings of frustration, of sadness, and of being lost on how to parent in the situation, and became shorter and snappier with not just Andrew but anyone who crossed my path during one of his outbursts.

Fast-forward to the end of the ten months, and "poof!" the fevers left just like that. I, of course, assumed (more like desperately hoped) that because they were gone that also "just like that" his speech would clear up, his screaming fits would clear up, and all my stress would clear up.

Well, it didn't.

Spending a good chunk of year two with a sore throat that hurt when he spoke hadn't really inspired Andrew to talk. It just inspired him to keep on yelling and, by default, it inspired me to keep on yelling, too.

Shortly after the fevers ended and the yelling started to actually intensify, I found myself huddled in a corner crying hysterically. I just couldn't take the screaming fits anymore. I just couldn't take another day of him throwing a sippy cup at me because he couldn't use any words. I just couldn't take another day of him banging his head against the wall because he couldn't talk. **I cried hysterically because I just couldn't take another day of feeling such anger toward my own son that I wanted to scream right back at him.**

I eventually pulled myself up from the floor.

I then walked into the kitchen, grabbed the phone, and finally accepted that I couldn't do this on my own. I dialed the speech therapist, whose number I had had for weeks but didn't call because I refused to accept that my son had a problem that I couldn't change.

Luckily for us, Rachelle, the speech therapist, came to Andrew's rescue. She loved him and worked with and got him to use his words. And let me tell you, the day he finally said, "Mommy, I luv you," my heart melted in a way that words cannot express. And the day he said to me, "Mommy. ORANGE RHINO!" … well, that day I cried tears of joy. Not only was he really using words, but he was also getting concepts and expressing them. It was a long and oftentimes painful journey waiting for Andrew to learn to talk and express himself. He is still making progress and still seeing Rachelle. And I am still making progress and still working to be patient with him during his screaming fits.

Every day I work to remind myself to accept the situation, to accept that I can't make the speech delay go away on my schedule, that I can't make the year plus of screaming training go away, that I can't make this struggle go away.

Every day I work to accept that Andrew is working hard to communicate, that he isn't throwing a screaming fit because he is trying to piss me off, but because it was his norm for so long and that it will take a long while to totally break the habit.

Every day I work to accept that our current norm is that Andrew might have a screaming fit in public, that he might yell longer and louder than I wish, that I might struggle to parent

So every day I remind myself to go with the flow by accepting the situation, to accept Andrew and his loud voice, to accept that things are harder than I wish.

effectively in said situations, and that I will definitely get sneered at, talked about, and potentially yelled at by onlookers.

Every day I try to embrace American author Robert Elias's quote, *"If you can't fight and you can't flee, flow."*

I don't want to fight my son when I know he is struggling, and I definitely don't want to flee him. I love him.

So every day I remind myself to go with the flow by accepting the situation, to accept Andrew and his loud voice, to accept that things are harder than I wish. Because when I do accept—really, really, accept the truth—those days are infinitely better and way easier to not yell unnecessarily at my sweet boy. Because on those days, I don't carry around anger. I just carry around unconditional love, empathy, and knowledge that we are both trying to do our best under the circumstances, and that is what really matters.

Orange Rhino Revelations

- I spend a lot of negative energy trying to change things that I can't; all that negative energy grows and gets me to a spot where I am not present with my kids and where just about anything will trigger me to want to yell.

- Learning to accept things that I cannot change is hard, but when I do, life is easier and full of more positive energy. When I accept the unchangeable triggers, my desire to yell goes down and the quality of my relationships with everyone in my life goes up.

Today's Actions

- **Accept the unchangeable triggers.** Revisit the trigger you focused on yesterday. Deepen your acceptance of it by stating simply over and over, "I cannot change (trigger), but I can change me." Say it 1,000 times if you need to until you believe it. Write it down on a sticky note and put it in your sock drawer if you need to start the day remembering it.

- **Write down two or three ways you can instantly change your attitude when this trigger arises.** Example: recalling positive memories associated with the person/ problem you have encountered, practicing gratitude, calling a friend.

- **Cry, let out the frustration, sadness, and disappointment if you need to** (which I did, and sometimes still do). Let it all out. Don't hold it in … that will eventually make you yell! Sometimes, this is what is needed to move on. Let yourself feel what you have been wanting to feel but have been afraid to acknowledge.

I know this action is a hard pill to swallow. I also know from my blog that everyone has at least one if not two triggers they would love to completely alleviate or at least learn to control that they can't. True, some things we just can't control, and that is frustrating. Accept that— as well as the fact that you can control your response—and that trigger will feel smaller.

> **66 Grant me the serenity to accept** the things I cannot change, the courage to change the things I can, and the wisdom to know the difference. **99**
>
> —Reinhold Niebuhr

Today's Tips

COOL	Pull out family photo album; trips down memory lane take everyone to a happy, smiley place.
WARM	Use sign language; my kids love when I use my secret silent code to ask them to do something. Why wouldn't they? It is way better than yelling demands!
	Tell yourself, "Hey, things could be worse," to gain perspective and gratitude for what you do have.
HOT	Put a finger over your mouth in the shhh position; this creates a physical barrier to yelling.

When we are feeling frustrated, I sign "I love you" to help us refocus on a happy thought so the negative ones (and behaviors!) take a hike.

Day 14

Practice Forgiveness:
I Dwell, Therefore I Yell

Okay, so um, wow, this chapter has been pretty heavy and deep so far, wouldn't you say? Hopefully this little story will lighten things up a bit and make you laugh. And yes, I fully expect to be laughed at; I'm cool with that.

Early on in The Orange Rhino Challenge when I had just started tracking triggers, I discovered that I seemed to always want to yell unnecessarily or more quickly than usual if my mind was preoccupied overthinking a problem, which, according to my tracking sheets, proved to be, um, a lot. Way more than a lot.

If things didn't go as planned, whether that means a birthday party, a vacation, a date night, or a family outing, then I dwelled on what was lost, what could have been better.

If I had a difficult conversation with my mom or an upsetting interaction with my son, then I dwelled on what took place and what I could have, should have done better and what I really wished hadn't been said or done to me.

If I didn't get done everything I had hoped for in the day or if I didn't finish something to my liking, especially a blog post, then I dwelled on my non-perfection.

If I had an email exchange with a friend and afterward felt sad that we weren't as in touch as before, or if I had a busy week and didn't have time to call or connect with friends and realized my disappointment about how hard it is to balance all the important things in life, then I dwelled on my insecurity of not being a good friend, wife, mom.

Yes, I was the Queen of Dwelling! I guess this wasn't entirely news. I had always known that I had a tendency to dwell. I just didn't realize (or want to realize?) that my tendency to dwell also created the tendency to want to yell, but oh, did it ever! If something negative happened to me, my immediate chain reaction was to think and think and think about it until my smallish feelings of frustration, hurt, annoyance, confusion, or disappointment became so large and omnipresent (or is it omnipotent?) that if any child dared to need me, pick a fight with a brother, or interrupt my self-induced dizzying state of negative thinking, then ROARRRRRR! Oh yes, dwelling made me charge with my words—big-time.

With this newfound realization, I began doing as I had trained myself in my early challenge days: I started thinking (okay, dwelling) about how I could manage this trigger. I found I had no clue; I had been a professional dweller for years, and I obviously had no idea how not to be one. Serendipitously, the day after I identified this trigger, I sat in a waiting room and stumbled upon a *Real Simple* magazine article about helping people stop bad habits. Given that I was currently trying to tackle the bad habit of yelling, I tore open the magazine and eagerly began reading the article.

The first habit tackled ruminating. My first thought? *"What the hell does ruminating mean?"*

My second thought after reading the introductory paragraph that described ruminating: *"Holy sh*t. There is a fancy term for the problem I struggle with. I am a Ruminator."*

And my third thought, because my brain always makes the oddest, most absurd connections, especially when silly words rhyme: *"I am the Sherminator ... you've been targeted for Shermination."*

Yep, here I sat reading a serious article with great points on how to help me stop ruminating and my mind wandered off and started thinking about Sherman from the *American Pie* movies and how he pretended to be the "Sherminator" instead of the "Terminator" to try and pick up girls.

> **It meant forgiving myself over and over and over again if I yelled at my kids, because without that forgiveness there was no moving forward. There was just feeling crappy and crappier and crappier about yelling, which just made me yell more and more and more.**

And while Sherman's pick-up line never really successfully helped him pick up girls, I will say that his line has been extremely successful at helping me stop ruminating and therefore stop yelling. Every time I find myself beginning to dwell, I now say to myself: *"I am the Ruminator ... a problem has been targeted for Rumination."*

And then I laugh. Because whenever I think of my line and by default, of Sherman, I can't help but say my line to myself—not in my voice, but in the Sherminator voice! My laughter reminds me that I don't really want to ruminate, that it triggers me to yell, and that I need to let go and move on; in other words, that I need to stop being the Ruminator and start being ... wait for it, wait for it ... the Terminator! Ah, I am such a tool! I hope you are smiling now or at least saying this line with me in a super-cool Terminator voice: "I am the Terminator ... Dwelling behavior has been targeted for Termination!"

Seriously, though, to stop yelling I had to start saying goodbye to being the Ruminator and hello to being the Terminator. I had to start forcing myself to stop thinking about the problem that had brought me down because it just made the problem seem worse. It put me in a worse mental state and, therefore, a worse place for my kids. This didn't just include letting go of negative interactions that happened with others, though. Oh no. It also included letting go and no longer ruminating on my negative interactions with myself.

It meant no longer criticizing myself over and over for not being thin enough.

It meant no longer telling myself over and over that I am not a good enough mom.

It meant no longer putting myself down over and over when I made a simple mistake, like snapping at my kids.

AND, it meant forgiving myself over and over and over again if I yelled at my kids, because without that forgiveness there was no moving forward. There was just feeling more crappy about yelling, which just made me yell more and more and more.

It took me several tries to master The Orange Rhino Challenge. I went eight-ish days the first go-around. And then I yelled. And then I dwelled on my mistake. And dwelled. And dwelled. I have no doubt that it was ruminating that kept me yelling, that kept me from moving forward toward my goal. C. S. Lewis described my problem perfectly: "Getting over a painful experience is much like crossing monkey bars. You have to let go at some point in order to move forward." But well, I just couldn't let go of "making a mistake" (you know, of being human!) or of my disappointment in myself. I just kept thinking and thinking of my mistake—and not in a positive, "How-can-I-fix-this-situation-and-create-a-positive-action-to-move-forward?" way, but in an "I so stink at this not-yelling-thing" way.

Needless to say, the more I dwell, the harder it is to terminate the ruminating thoughts. I needed to accept that I am human and that I might make a mistake such as yelling too much. So accept I did.

The day I snapped was the day I finally became able to embrace that I was working my butt off; that day, instead of dwelling on my faults, I celebrated that I had at least gone eight days not yelling, and that it was all good. That day, I finally stopped ruminating about "the yell that broke my streak" and I forgave myself. And that day turned out to be Day 1 of my successful completion of 365 days of not yelling.

66 One cannot too soon forget his errors and misdemeanors; for to dwell upon them is to add to the offense. **99**

—Henry David Thoreau

Day 14: Revelations, Actions, and Tips

Orange Rhino Revelations

- "Should have" is a dangerous phrase; it fosters dwelling and therefore yelling. "Next time, I will..." is a more positive phrase.
- Dwelling, like yelling, makes things worse.
- **Focusing on the negatives in my life makes it hard to see the positives in anyone, especially my kids. When I see negative, I am more likely to speak negatively.**
- I readily forgive others for mistakes, but I do not readily forgive myself, and I need to.

Today's Actions

- **Practice forgiveness.** Forgive yourself for all past yells. Practice saying out loud—yes, out loud because you would say it out loud to a friend—"I forgive me for yelling in the past. Mistakes happen. I am only human."
- **Let go of the unchangeable trigger if you haven't already.** For me, this meant not focusing on it as much, but focusing on my behavior and response to it. If I feel the need to vent about an annoyance, I do it so that my tension doesn't grow. But, I now actively work to minimize the amount of time I allow for negative thoughts. Then I force myself to focus on positive thoughts and solutions.

Today's Tips

COOL	Start blowing bubbles; this reminds me of being a child and how I worried less then and that I should let go and chill out. (It also helps slow your breathing and heart rate down!)
WARM	If help is around, tag out. Letting go of control and asking for help is huge. If you can't tag out, then play tag with the kids. The exercise will help you let go of the desire to yell.
HOT	Shake your body, arms, and legs—you know, kind of like how you tell the kids to shake the sillies out? Shake the stress and yells out!

Dear Orange Rhino in the making,

I just wanted to take a moment to write a note of encouragement to you because I know the journey to stop yelling is hard! I know how tempting it is to quit, especially if change isn't coming as fast as you'd like. Oh, do I know this! But please, don't give up on yourself, the journey, or the process. You can do this. Just by the mere fact that you are this far into the book proves how determined you are to change. Hold tight to that determination and let it and the love for your kids keep pushing you toward change. It will happen. Maybe not on the timetable you wish, but it will happen. Anytime you are feeling down about your progress, think of my new favorite quote that I discovered on my journey which kept me going:

"Victory is not won in miles, but in inches. Win a little now, hold your ground, and later, win a little more." —Louis L'Amour

And as you keep reading, please remember these four really important things:
- If you yell, it doesn't mean you are a failure, it just means you learned something new about what doesn't work.
- You do not stink at this—you are like all of us who work daily to improve.
- You are doing better than you realize—realizing that you want to change and trying is a big step, a big step forward.
- You are a great person and parent who shows up every day and does your best.

Thinking of you and sending good vibes your way,

—The Orange Rhino

4

Prepare to Charge Forward

One important key to success is self-confidence. An important key to self-confidence is preparation.

—Arthur Ashe

At this point, you know that it took me several tries to go 365 consecutive days without yelling. And you know that one of the keys that finally stopped me from having to restart is that I forgave myself for my "mistake yells." The other key? February 7, 2012, the first morning of my successful 365-day stretch, I woke up and no longer doubted myself. When I started the challenge, I succeeded because I ran on adrenaline and the desire to prove everyone wrong who doubted me. But that feeling only lasted so long and pretty much disappeared when, after eight days, I yelled. Suddenly, I doubted myself. That doubt, coupled with the inability to let go of my "mistake yells," kept me from succeeding. But that morning in February I so clearly remember waking up and feeling confident because I realized that all the days before had prepared me to succeed.

All the good days taught me what worked to keep calm, what I needed to stay calm, and how I needed to stay calm. And all the not-so-good days taught me what definitely didn't work! This sudden new realization made me feel prepared to take on any new challenges thrown my way because I knew I had the tools and the experience to conquer them. Tennis great Arthur Ashe's quote couldn't be more accurate, which is why I suggest that before you officially go after the *Yell Less, Love More* challenge you spend the next three days doing "final preparations" to build your confidence and set you up for success.

Day 15

Choose a Personal Goal:
If I Can Just Make It to 9:05 a.m. ...

There is no eloquent, Martha Stewart–appropriate way to write this: Every single school morning used to be (and sometimes still can be) an absolute sh*t storm in our house. As I wrote earlier, I am just not a morning person. I take about two hours to wake up and get with the program, which is about two hours too late. Even on nights when I get a good night's sleep, I still struggle to get a good groove going in the morning. So I am irritable. Wicked, wicked irritable. And yes, you guessed it: This makes it very hard to stay calm and yell-free during the morning rush of trying to get breakfast on the table, lunches packed, and bodies out the door with empty bladders and shoes on both feet all while trying to keep peace between the boys who overnight seemed to have forgotten how to play nicely. I mean, really, I swear every morning starts with reteaching my boys the basics of humanity! Okay, well not every morning, that is unfair; it's more like a couple of mornings a week.

One totally awful, absolutely horrific, unbelievably difficult morning my husband called and ever so innocently asked me, "Hey, how is the morning going?" **I burst into tears and cried, "I just can't do it! I just can't do it anymore. I hate the mornings! They are so hard! I'm going to bloody lose it any second! Forget The Orange Rhino Challenge! I quit!"**

Always my rock when motherhood pushed me to the edge, he said, "What time is it?"

"What do you mean?" I barked. "That's a stupid question. It's 8:27 here. Just like it is in your office."

"Okay. It's 8:27. When do you leave for school?"

"8:50."

"Okay. And how many kids do you drop off then?"

"Three. You know that. Why are you asking these dumb questions?"

"And when are you home with Mac for his nap?"

"9:05."

"Okay. So all you have to do is make it to 8:50. That is 23 minutes. You can do that. In 23 minutes the kids will be buckled in and unable to touch each other."

"Uh huh," I sobbed, wiping snot from my nose as someone wiped breakfast on my leg.

"And then you just need to make it to 9:05 when Mac goes down for a nap. That is only 15 minutes more. Then you have quiet time for almost two hours to wake up and get ready to restart the day on a better note."

"Uh huh."

"Twenty-three minutes, babe. Then 15 minutes. Then it is 9:05. You can do this. You got this."

He was totally right. I could do this. It was a measurable, attainable goal. I can do anything for a mere 23 minutes and then a mere 15 minutes. I just kept telling myself over and over and over that I just had to make it to 9:05. I didn't need to worry about not yelling all day. I didn't need to worry about not yelling for 10 hours and 33 minutes. I just needed to focus on not yelling for 38 minutes. Thirty-eight minutes. I could do that. That is so much more of a manageable task and inspiring goal than 10 hours and 33 minutes!

Well, wouldn't you know, I did it! I made it through that morning without yelling … kind of. The minute the minivan door slammed shut and my last munchkin walked into school, I yelled out such a loud and enthusiastic "PHEW!" that the teacher turned to see if everything was okay. Oops! Of course everything was okay, it was better than okay! I had survived a hellacious morning without yelling and felt wicked proud! I had been so tempted that morning to say, "Screw it, it doesn't matter if I yell," but instead I busted my ass to keep it together. I went home, put Mr. Mac down for his nap, and then celebrated by enjoying the peace and quiet of the house while drinking my nice cup of cold coffee that I never got to drink that morning. (Side note: Have I ever had a cup of hot coffee since having kids?! Or at least one that wasn't microwaved five or six times?! Um, no.)

The rest of the day went surprisingly well given the very rocky start. In fact, it went so smoothly that I don't recall any more moments of calling my husband in tears or wanting to quit. I do, however, recall and now daily rely on, two phenomenal conclusions that I came to that night as I sat plopped on my couch, relishing the peace and quiet (with a cup of HOT decaf coffee) and the fact that I had made it through another entire day not yelling. All cozied up with no one to interrupt me and no negative thoughts to ruminate over, I found myself pondering how the heck I made it through the day without yelling. I mean, yes, I knew my husband had helped, but I felt the need to try and figure out what else, if anything, had helped me so that I could call on my newfound secret powers the next morning.

This is what I realized almost immediately: I had no real secret powers. This was kind of a total bummer; it would have been cool to have magic powers to make me not yell. That just would have made life WAY easier. But alas, I did get some power in realizing these two facts:

First: On days when I stay calm enough to get to 9:05 a.m. without yelling, and I therefore send the kids off to school with love in their hearts (and minds) instead of anger and mean sentiments, the day goes smoother. Starting out the day on a good note is good for all of us. It not only fills me with confidence that I can indeed not yell, but it also fills my kids with happiness and connection, which I do believe helps them listen better, which makes not yelling easier.

Second: Realizing that just focusing on making it to 9:05 a.m. and not 7:00 p.m. without yelling made the entire challenge of not yelling feel that much easier. I knew my goal of going 365 days straight with not yelling helped me on a larger scale by providing me with a tangible and motivational goal. However, I will not lie; at times it did feel daunting. Understandably, right?! I mean 365 days multiplied by 14 hours—well, that is a lot of hours of not yelling. But 365 days multiplied by just the three hours before school— well, that is a lot more doable.

The next day, I took these two, new powerful insights and started breaking my day down into smaller pieces. Yes, I maintained my long-term goal of 365 days, but I also set smaller

> Yes, I maintained my long-term goal of 365 days, but I also set smaller goals: Get through breakfast. Get through getting ready for school. Get through the hyperactivity that comes with coming home from school.

goals: Get through breakfast. Get through getting ready for school. Get through the hyperactivity that comes with coming home from school. Get through homework. Get through dinner. Get through bath. Setting small goals to help me achieve my big goal made the overwhelming thought of, *"Argh, I just have to get through this day"* into, *"Okay, right now I only have to get through this moment."* And by adopting the latter statement, I easily and naturally started saying, "Wow, I totally got through this day!"

A few days later my husband asked me how the mornings were going. Being one stubborn lady, I didn't want to admit to him that his "just get to 9:05" advice had been a total game changer. You know, I didn't want to admit to him that he was right. Have I mentioned that I am stubborn?! So instead I replied with, "Mornings are going much better. Your advice the other morning made me think of my favorite quotation by Herb Kelleher that I talk about all the time: *'Think small and act small, and we'll get bigger. Think big and act big, and we'll get smaller.'* I had been trying to go big or go home—you know, focusing on going the whole day without yelling. But I started focusing on one small moment at a time and then it has been easier. And the small moments grow and add up and end up being a full day."

"Oh, so you mean my 'just get to 9:05' advice was good."

"Yeah, I guess so."

"So I was right?" my husband said, smirking.

"Yes dear, you were right," I said gratefully.

Even though a very small, small part of me hated that he was right, all the rest of me felt nothing but immense gratitude. I was grateful that he shared his advice, and that I listened. I was grateful that I figured out to go one moment at a time, not just in the morning, but all day. I was grateful that I realized that hitting small goals counted as success because those achievements would help me get to the big goal. And I was most definitely grateful that I wasn't taking this challenge alone, that my husband was by my side, supporting me, helping me reach my goal.

Day 15: Revelations, Actions, and Tips

Orange Rhino Revelations

- Both mini and big goals kept me on task.
- Achievement of my mini goals throughout the day gave me confidence to get through the rest of the day.
- My big goal gave me the push and encouragement to keep going day after day.

Today's Actions

- **Choose a big personal goal.** Using your notes from tracking your triggers and using your feelings about how hard this journey has been for you thus far, choose a personal goal that is reflective of *your own yelling situation* and that inspires you big-time, scares you a little, and incorporates what I learned in college about goal setting (and confirmed by Wikipedia because I forgot one element). Goals should be S.M.A.R.T.:

  - ▸ **Specific:** Be as detailed as possible.

  - ▸ **Measurable:** Use concrete criteria so that you can easily track your progress.

  - ▸ **Attainable:** Pick a goal that is difficult enough to make you work hard and push yourself out of your comfort zone, but that is realistic given your resources.

  - ▸ **Relevant:** I know yelling less is relevant to you because I know you love your kids, so this part is already achieved. Well done!

  - ▸ **Time-bound:** Set a time by which you want your goal achieved (e.g., one month, three months).

- **Break down your big goal into smaller pieces.**

  - ▸ **Choose a small goal to start on your path to the big goal to build confidence.** (I missed this piece; if I had done it earlier, it would have taken away some stress!) A popular suggestion The Orange Rhino community liked was to choose five "popular" easy and manageable triggers that happened a lot. Focus on one and try removing it within one week. When it is under control, cross it off and go to the next, and so on. When all five are under control, go for the big goal.

  - ▸ **Brainstorm some mini goals to help you get to the small goal** (e.g., get to 9:05 a.m.). Review your trigger tracking sheets for ideas.

- **Examples of goals set by Orange Rhinos:**
  - Go 30 days straight without yelling at all (small goal: 1 week).
  - Go 1 month only yelling once a day instead of 12 times a day (as shown on tracking sheet); when achieved, go 3 months without yelling (big goal).
  - Go 1 week straight without yelling, then 2 weeks, then 4 weeks, then 8 weeks, and so on.
  - Go 365 days without yelling (small goal: 10 days, then 100 days).
- **Decide how you will measure your goal.** Seeing your success fuels more success and reminds you that you can do it, because you did do it! Whatever you choose, be creative and make sure you place your "goal counter" somewhere highly visible. Every time you succeed you might:
  - Place orange hearts, stickers, or smiley faces on a calendar.
  - Add an orange object, such as an orange M&M, pom-pom, or glass bead to a clear glass vase.
  - Put a quarter (or more!) in a clear bucket to buy a reward for yourself at the end.
  - Post an orange note with the message "Day 1, I did it!"
- **Write your goal down on paper and share it with your support network.** I encourage you to physically write it down; don't just type it!

Remember, this is YOUR goal, and only you know how hard you need to push yourself to be motivated; only you know your personality and whether an all-or-nothing goal such as 365 days straight would motivate you or overwhelm you. If your goal feels way too scary and not exciting, it is probably too much. If it feels easy-peasy, push yourself to reach higher. Remember, as motivational speaker Les Brown says, "Shoot for the moon and if you miss you will still be among the stars." Seriously. Aim high; what's the worst that can happen? You are yelling less than before? That is a win!

> **66** **Any person who selects a goal in life**
> which can be fully achieved has
> already defined his own limitations. **99**
>
> —Cavett Robert

Today's Tips

COOL	Change your passwords to ones that remind you of your goal (e.g., Iwillyellless).
WARM	Ask yourself before you yell, "Wait, were my directions S.M.A.R.T.?"
HOT	Start running in place with the goal of getting the fight-or-flight impulse out of your system.

Day 16

Create Positive Affirmations:
The Vicious—I Mean *Victorious*—Cycle

I like to play games with my kids. Whether it is playing Uno; Sorry; Connect 4; or Hungry, Hungry, Hippos, I could sit and play all afternoon, just like I did when I was a kid. There is only one game that I just really can't stand playing at all. It isn't a board game, or a card game, or any other type of game I played as a child. Nope. Instead, it is a game that my son and I created on our own. Unfortunately, even though I hate playing it, and I know that he equally hates playing it, we seem to play it a lot. And we really struggle to stop playing it, which is a shame because it is a huge yelling trigger.

The name of the game? I have affectionately called it "The Vicious Cycle." And I play it with not just one son, but with all my sons and, it turns out, with my husband too.

Here's how it works.

My son and I both have to be in bad moods at the same time. Once we are both sufficiently stressed and anxious, sometimes for the same reasons, sometimes not, we quickly get stuck being impatient, rude, and quite frankly, annoying toward each other. My son starts acting out: yelling at me more, crying more, listening less, and smiling less. I start acting out, too: snapping more, yelling more, listening less, engaging less, and smiling less. His behavior makes me act out more, and when I act out more, he acts out more, which, of course, makes me act out even more, and so on and so forth. It is a vicious, and I mean VICIOUS cycle. The objective is to see how long we can spiral out of control before one of us gets so bad that the other one gives in and starts being nice enough to break the cycle.

Sounds like an awesome game, right? UGH. It sucks and it's a pain in the ass because it is exhausting, physically and mentally. Why can't he pull it together? Why can't I pull it together? Darn it, I didn't sleep again last night because I am so stressed. Darn it, he didn't sleep either because he is so unnerved by how I am acting in general and toward him. Crap, now we are both tired and even more overwhelmed and persnickety and even more likely to make the game continue another day, as well as play it harder.

At the start of the vicious cycle, I try my hardest to stay calm, patient, loving, and understanding so that I can keep us from spiraling out of control. I try not to take my son's actions personally; I try to help him in the ways I have learned, but I struggle. My problem? My stress is often so great at the time that I can't do what he needs me to do: be calm, patient, loving, and understanding.

One time during The Orange Rhino Challenge we were engaged in an awesome game; awesome in the sense that it was lasting close to a couple of weeks, awesome in that I ended it, and awesome that I had a great takeaway from it. I wrote on my blog:

> I was really close to losing it and yelling at him. Really, really close. I had had it with the screaming and the nasty attitude. I had had it with feeling like I was the only parent to have a child act like this. I had had enough of ALL OF IT. I had had it with my week, with my stress. I had had it with him. I was done being patient. I was done being The Orange Rhino. I walked away to type my frustration on The Orange Rhino Facebook page so I didn't scream it at him. I saw my logo and was immediately reminded of my promise to my boys to love more and to myself to not yell. I stopped typing, looked at him, and said, "What is wrong? Why are you so angry? Why are you throwing pillows at me?"
>
> My son burst into tears.
>
> "I am scared we are going to be in a car accident again. I am mad Daddy works so much. And I am angry that the babysitter left. Why doesn't she love me anymore?"
>
> Ouch. My son felt so much pain and I was in so much pain that I hadn't stopped to reach out to him, to understand him, to love him. Double ouch. I held him in my arms so tight and rocked him like a baby. He crumpled into my lap and arms and sat and cried and cried and cried. Those tears kicked me in the ass. Those tears reminded me that when in a vicious cycle with him, **he needs me. I am the one responsible for ending the cycle. I am the adult. I am the one who, no matter how hard it is, needs to find the strength and patience to give my son what he needs to "snap out of it." I am the one who needs to stop and ask, what is going on?**
>
> When my son is in a bad mood, rightfully or wrongfully, I need to keep on loving him. When my son is struggling, I need to be an Orange Rhino. I need to find warmth and composure. I need to be patient and calm. I need to be understanding.
>
> When my son and I are in a vicious cycle of bringing each other down, I have two choices: make it worse or make it better. I finally made it better. It took me days to realize this, it took me days to GROW UP and realize my son needed me. But at least I finally did. And not just because it kept me from yelling, but because it allowed me to love my son more. **And really, that is all he needed. To be loved more.**

And really, that is also all I need. To be loved more. By myself.

Sadly, I don't play this game, The Vicious Cycle, just with my sons and my husband, but I also play it with myself, just in a slightly different manner. My vicious cycle with myself is all about telling myself negative thoughts such as, *"I can't lose weight,"* and *"No one likes me,"* and *"There is no way I will be able to stop yelling."* The way my personal game works is that I say these negative thoughts over and over and over again, until I have said them so many times that I believe them and they actually come true. Then I have "won," although obviously, I have really lost.

I have lost faith in myself that I can do hard things.

I have lost courage to believe that I can accomplish what I set out to.

I have lost control over my ability to easily manage my desire to not yell.

> ## That said, this challenge proved to me that the more positive I am with my thoughts about what I can achieve, the more I achieve.

When I get stuck in my vicious cycle of negative self-talk, I set myself up to want to yell and scream to let out my personal pain, frustration, and disappointment.

Yes, I lose a lot when I think negatively. In fact, all I gain is a self-fulfillment of exactly what I tried to avoid in the first place. When I started The Orange Rhino Challenge, anytime someone said something to me along the lines of "oh, the power of positive thinking," I rolled my eyes, struggling to totally believe the cliché. Yes, I do believe in being positive and I do believe it helps, but I didn't believe it was the "be-all and end-all" to solving problems and overcoming challenges. And I still don't believe it is; I am a realist.

That said, this challenge proved to me that the more positive I am with my thoughts about what I can achieve, the more I achieve. The days that I say to myself, *"I can do this. I will choose to love more and yell less,"* are infinitely easier and more successful than the ones where I say, *"ARGH! I can't do this!"* Thinking positively does help me achieve more positive results; it is very contagious.

And being a realist, and from playing The Vicious Cycle more times than I care to admit, I can say that sometimes it is outright hard to think positively! It is hard to stop being mad at my son for his behavior and it is hard to stop being mad at myself for my behavior. But choosing to think positive thoughts toward myself and show positive behavior toward my son—well, it is necessary if I don't want to yell. So no matter how hard it is to accept responsibility for stopping The Vicious Cycle, whether it is with my sons or with myself, I will keep trying so that we can start playing The Victorious Cycle game of loving ourselves, each other, and life more.

 **Day 16: Revelations, Actions, and Tips**

Orange Rhino Revelations

- Learning to speak to myself positively, and filling my soul with positive thoughts, took hard work, practice, determination, and at times, sheer willpower, but the benefits were and continue to be powerful.

- Encouraging myself in my head by saying *"You can yell less and love more"* or *"You can do this"* feels silly sometimes, but it is absolutely necessary and helpful.

Today's Actions

- **Create positive affirmations.** Write down three or four positive affirmations using as much positive, in-the-present, passionate language as possible. Examples:

  ▸ I am a calm, loving parent who is in control of my voice.

  ▸ I am yelling less. I am an Orange Rhino.

  ▸ I am loving more, one moment at a time.

  ▸ I can do this! I will not yell! I love my kids! (This doesn't follow the suggested affirmation rules many people talk about *but* it worked for me because it centered me, reminded me of my goal, and was in the language I normally use.)

- **Say your affirmations to yourself all day and every day** and especially when you feel a yell trying to come out.

- **Post affirmations in key places** such as the bathroom mirror, car dashboard, and fridge.

66 **It's the repetition of affirmations that leads** to belief. And once that belief becomes a deep conviction, things begin to happen. **99**

—Muhammad Ali

Today's Tips

COOL	**Orange Rhino Favorite:** Write down this quotation by Gandhi on an orange piece of paper and read it over and over until you fully embrace it: "A man is but the product of his thoughts; what he thinks, he becomes."
WARM	Bite tongue (gently, of course) and talk; you'll sound like you have marshmallows in your mouth and everyone will laugh, defusing the situation.
HOT	Say, "Serenity now," or whatever your mantra is. My most popular one is, "I am an Orange Rhino!"

Day 17

Take Care of Yourself: Sleep, Eat, Run, Clean ... Poop?

When James started first grade, he went from going to school three hours a day to seven hours a day. Needless to say, the adjustment rattled him. He did fabulous during school, but the minute he rolled in from school, *"Whoa, Nellie!"* One afternoon in the beginning of the year I decided to be proactive. We shared the following conversation.

Me: "So, James, it seems that after school we need to help you unwind from your long day. What do you think you can do to take care of yourself so that you can have an enjoyable afternoon at home?"

James: "I don't know. But I need to go poop. Okay?"

Me: "Um, okay." And then to myself, *"Okay son, um, good chat?"*

After James had entered the bathroom and sat down he said to me through the closed door, "So, Mom, I am not really pooping. I am just sitting on the toilet trying to poop. I find it to be very calming, actually. You know, a small, quiet room with no disturbances and just focusing on one thing: pooping. You should try it someday. You might actually like it more than I do."

I couldn't stop laughing after he said that. He was probably right—focusing on just one thing? That would be fantastic! Having a room that is quiet? Oh, how glorious! Having both those things at once? Heck, that would be calming! But that just isn't an option for me. When I go to the bathroom, I normally have one child in with me, one knocking at the door, one trying to open the door, and the other one yelling at me to "hurry up already, I need to go peeeee!"

Yes, going to the bathroom is so *not* how I calm down. But, I still appreciated the good laugh from my son and the insight into what helps him find calm: a quiet room, a singular focus, and time to himself. This was huge. The next day we translated that insight into having him go straight to his room after school to quietly build LEGO masterpieces, by himself, until he felt relaxed enough to come peacefully hang with the family. Knowing his recipe for getting to a calm place, both in the heat of the moment and as a preventative measure, has worked wonders. Wonders!

It only took me a couple of years and a frank conversation about pooping to figure out James's "Recipe for Calm," as I now like to call it. This is actually quite impressive given it took me, let's see, how old was I when I started The Orange Rhino Challenge? Right, thirty-four. It took me thirty-four years to really figure out my Recipe for Calm and that's only because I had no choice *but* to figure it out if I wanted to succeed at not yelling! Tracking my triggers had quickly showed me that on days when I felt stressed or unhappy, that my chances of staying calm enough not to yell when a tough moment arose, were small—like, really, really small.

It was an eye-opening experience for me to realize that so much of my ability to not yell didn't just depend on my ability to keep calm *during* tough moments, as expected, but also

> My ability to not yell didn't just depend on my ability to keep calm *during* tough moments, as expected, but also on my ability to daily take care of myself so that I was in a calm, relaxed place *well before* those tempting-to-yell moments.

on my ability to daily take care of myself so that I was in a calm, relaxed place *well before* those tempting-to-yell moments. This way, when those moments did arise, I would have the inner resilience to handle them without yelling. You know what else was eye-opening? When I realized what a crucial role "taking care of me" played in not yelling, I also sadly realized that I didn't really know anymore *how* to take care of me. I didn't know what I enjoyed doing to relax or what worked for me as a quick pick-me-up on days when I felt "blech." I just didn't really understand myself anymore. I didn't really know what helped get me to a calm, good place because it had been so long since I had actively prioritized myself, since I had actually put "Take care of me" on the to-do list.

Ever since I became a mom, I stopped taking care of me. In fact, I refused to take care of me. I refused to do things that relaxed me. I refused to do things that made me happy. Instead, I convinced myself that to be a good mom, I had to put my kids' needs above all of mine. I convinced myself that I couldn't do the things I liked to do, such as organize and clean, because I should spend all my time with my kids. I convinced myself that taking time for me to go to the gym or to talk to a girlfriend was selfish. I convinced myself that even if I wanted to take time for myself, there wasn't time because there were too many other more important things to do. You know what, though? Turns out that I couldn't do those other important things, such as loving my kiddos and not yelling at them, if I operated on empty, if I didn't regularly do things that made me happy and calm. **I needed to take care of me so that I could take care of my family.** And I needed to relearn what the heck that meant!

A lot of thinking, a lot of trial and error, and *a lot* of rereading my trigger tracking sheets to figure out what I didn't do on days when it was hard to find calm, led me to five things (beyond quality time with the fam) that belonged on my new, "take care of me list."

1. Eat well. On days when I ate too much junk food, and my body felt bloated and gross, I felt cranky, disappointed in myself, fat, and on edge. And if I didn't eat, then, oy vey, did I ever feel cranky and on edge! Food had a way bigger impact on my desire to yell than I cared to admit and needed major attention.

2. Get more sleep. Before James was born, I needed at least eight hours of sleep to be a pleasant person. That need didn't changed when James was born and actually, it just grew in necessity as our family grew in size. What did change though was that eight hours became a luxury and six hours became the reality ... because I let it. Night after night I told myself, *"Eh, sleep doesn't matter. I'll catch up some night."* Well, that some night never happened; all that happened was I became more tired, more snappy with my boys, less calm, and way more prone to want to yell. My lack of sleep was making me, and therefore my kiddos, miserable and I couldn't ignore that it was deeply affecting my ability to remain calm enough to not yell.

3. Exercise whenever possible. Before The Orange Rhino Challenge, I knew exercise made me happy. I didn't realize to what extent though until I noticed that on days when I didn't exercise, not yelling was very, very hard and on days when I did get my body moving, whether with formal exercise, a walk outside, or a dance party with my boys, that I was much, much calmer and not yelling was much, *much* easier.

4. Be social and connect with friends. I had no idea how much talking, laughing, and just hanging with my friends—even if just for a few moments a day after drop offs, helped me be in a good, calm, place until well, I had less and less of those interactions due to our crazy family schedule. Scratch that. It was due to the fact that I didn't make socializing a priority because I didn't realize its importance, because I didn't realize that my social needs were just as important as my boys'.

5. Clean and organize. Cleaning my kitchen calms me down. Vacuuming makes me happy. A disorganized, dirty home, dirty dishes, and clutter *do not.* They make me stressed! I know there are sayings along the lines of "The dishes will always be there, but precious moments with kids will not." And I totally get the sentiment, which is why I used to feel wicked guilty when I chose cleaning the real ceramic dishes covered in spaghetti sauce over cleaning the fake plastic dishes covered in hot fudge and ketchup with my two year old. During the challenge, though, I realized that it is OKAY to want to clean the real dishes. It is okay to want to be productive and cross things off my personal to-do list in order to stay calm. It is okay to need to be productive in order to get calm. **It is more than okay to say, "I need to do something for ME in order to be there for my kids and not yell at them."**

Before The Challenge, I felt guilty and sometimes embarrassed not just when I chose the dishes over my kids, but also when I chose to exercise instead of doing Play-Doh; when I chose to ask Grandma to put the kids to bed instead of me so I could grab dinner with a friend; when I chose to go to bed early instead of making the already "more than good enough birthday cupcakes" perfect. Before The Challenge I got so wrapped up in worrying about what a good mom supposedly does (or doesn't do) that I actually stopped being a good mom because I started following some *other* mom's "recipe for calm" instead of my *own.*

The Orange Rhino Challenge forced me to stop feeling guilty about what makes *me* calm and happy and to instead feel proud that not only did I finally figure out my personal "recipe for calm," but also that I finally found the courage to embrace and follow it. When days are tough, whether because of the kids or because of my life, and I find myself feeling cranky and on edge, I push myself to stop and take care of me. I think of my "recipe for calm" and do something on it … and then I find that yelling less and loving more is much easier.

Day 17: Revelations, Actions, and Tips

Orange Rhino Revelations

- **Taking care of me is not selfish; it is actually one of the best gifts I can give my children.**

- Taking care of me doesn't need to be a big event; it can be as short as five minutes looking at pictures on my camera or as long as two hours out to dinner with friends.

Today's Actions

- **Take care of yourself.** Brainstorm all the things you wish you could do to take care of yourself to find a calm, happy place. Don't give excuses why they wouldn't work, even if it's tempting (e.g., don't have child care, don't have enough time, don't know how to make it happen). Think of both small and big things—dare to dream! (Rumor has it that just dreaming about doing something is calming!)

- **Create your Recipe for Calm** by picking about five things from your taking-care-of-me list. Be sure to include one or two that can be done daily in a short amount of time (e.g., listening to your favorite radio station, going for a walk), one or two that are a little more fulfilling (e.g., drinking a hot coffee out and about *without* kids), and one to work toward that requires planning and probably asking for help (e.g., an afternoon away with your husband).

- **Write your Recipe for Calm on a notecard and keep it handy.** When you feel you are at the end of your rope and ready to yell, you can refer to it to help you hold on and climb back up to a better place—without yelling!

" In the event of an emergency,
please put on your oxygen
mask first before assisting others. **"**

—Airline safety guidelines

– Or –

" I am taking care of me,
so I can take care of them. **"**

—Orange Rhino terms

Today's Tips

COOL	Light a candle at known bad times. I now light aromatherapy candles at bath time and pretend to be at the spa. Added bonus? It relaxes kids, too!
WARM	**Orange Rhino Favorite:** Stop everything and play with your kids; not only is this fun and a great stress reliever but sometimes this connection is just the thing that's needed!
HOT	Open up the freezer and put your head in and freeze that thought, literally and figuratively. Enjoy a good group laugh afterward!

Chill out—really! The cold air freezes me in the moment, helping me to focus on warming up my thoughts.

5

Start to Yell Less, and Love More

To accomplish great things, we must not only act, but also dream; not only plan, but also believe.

—Anatole France

I can say with all my heart and soul that teaching myself to stop yelling has changed my life. It has changed who I am as a mom, a wife, a daughter, a friend, and a neighbor. It has changed how I experience life, for the better. It has changed how I handle frustrations and fears; I now do so with much more confidence, maturity, insight, and strength. I would not have achieved this life-changing experience had I not dared to *dream* that I could change, had I not *believed* that I could change, had I not made a *plan* to change, and had I not finally *focused* to make it happen. At this point in the book, you have also already done these things! You have already dared to dream, you have already practiced and made a plan, and hopefully you have come to believe that you can accomplish great things. If you are still questioning whether or not you can, know this: I believe you can. I believe we all can change and make our dreams reality and I believe you are ready to do just that.

I know it may sound corny, but I am honest and sincere when I say that this chapter represents the start to a new chapter in your life. So here's to you and all the hard work you've done so far to prepare yourself to successfully turn the page to a new, wonderfully rewarding chapter.

Day 18

Becoming an Orange Rhino:
My Out-of-Body-Experience

Many a time on my journey I had moments where I responded to previously difficult situations with such a newfound sense of calm, grace, perspective, and control that I felt as if I was having an out-of-body experience. Seriously.

There was one time when I had the distinct pleasure of hearing a woman sitting right next to my husband and me at a restaurant make fun of us to her boyfriend for discussing a detailed reward system for our kiddos using golden doubloons like those in *Jake and the Neverland Pirates*.

Her: "What losers. They are out without kids and they are talking about reward systems."

Him: "Shhh. You're talking loud. They can hear you."

Her: "I don't care. Wait, do I lose two gold doubloons for being rude? Or is it one?"

Him: "Shhh. Please. It's embarrassing."

Her: "Honey, you get one gold doubloon for saying please. Would you like two gold doubloons for taking a bite of food?"

Oh, did my insecurity trigger fire up! Oh, did I want to burst into tears right then and there. Oh, did I want to tell her off and wish upon her years of difficult parenting. But I didn't. Instead, I told myself to let it go, that dwelling does me no good and would just ruin a peaceful night out with my hubby. So I wiped the tears out of my eyes, kept my cool, let go as fast as I could, and enjoyed my night on the town. I never, ever would have done that pre–Orange Rhino Challenge. Never, ever.

And then there was the time in Friendly's restaurant when I had all four kids by myself to celebrate James's birthday and Andrew had a sensory meltdown to end all meltdowns because his shirt got wet and he just couldn't cope. After removing him from the table and working my best to dry his shirt, an older woman said to me, "Why don't you bring him over here. I'll hit him for you and then take care of him. I'll make him shut up!"

I wanted to hit her with a bunch of nasty, insulting words and thoughts for indirectly insulting my parenting and for threatening to hurt my child. But I didn't. Instead, because I didn't want to ruin my son's celebration, without blinking an eye, I ever so sweetly and politely replied, "Oh, please don't talk to my son that way. It isn't nice and it isn't funny. He is a child. Both he and I are trying our hardest."

I never would have done that pre–Orange Rhino Challenge. Never, ever.

These out-of-body-experiences didn't just happen at times when I wanted to yell at strangers. One happened when I found myself not obsessing over making something perfect, but instead decided that good enough was better than enough. And one happened when I went to bed hours earlier than usual because I needed to take a "me night," instead of cracking the whip at my to-do list. Another happened when I found myself telling all the positive stories about my kids to my husband at night, instead of focusing on all the

> I started to no longer grow anger, resentment, frustration, or disappointment throughout the day, as I had done before The Orange Rhino Challenge. Instead, I started to grow more happiness, satisfaction, calm, and peace, and therefore, I started to grow a more fulfilling life.

frustrating ones first. And yet another happened when I found myself staring at my child, thoroughly enjoying the moment and every detail of his precious little face instead of worrying about everything I had to do. Yes, these out-of-body experiences happened a lot during The Orange Rhino Challenge and often startled, even scared, my husband and me.

One in particular really got him. We arrived at the beach for our annual summer vacation. It rained the first three days (awesome) and then on the fourth day when it stopped raining, we discovered that our favorite beach had shut down for renovations because of Hurricane Sandy. We had to go to a more-crowded, more-rowdy, farther-away-from-the-bathrooms beach. Boo! The old me would have sulked all week and complained whenever possible how my expectations weren't met and how disappointed I was. But I didn't. Instead, I went with the flow and focused on enjoying what I did have: time with my family at a beach. I never, ever, would have done that pre–Orange Rhino Challenge. Never, ever. In fact, I shocked my husband so much with my response to the situation that he asked me, "Who are you and what have you done with my wife?"

It was a totally legitimate question! To say that handling myself this way in this moment (and all previously mentioned ones) is a drastic turnaround for me is an absolute understatement. The change is so profound that it is almost frightening. At times after one of these out-of-body-holy-sh*t-I-have-totally-changed-this-is-surreal moments, I have even said to myself, *"Who is this person responding like this? Where is the Sheila I knew? Did I change that much just because of The Orange Rhino Challenge?"*

The answer to myself was always an emphatic *"YES!"* followed by, *"Wowsers, I can't believe how much this challenge has changed my life in ways I never expected."* And then, of course, *"Wow, I am such a sap."*

And I am. **Whenever one of these moments hits and proves to me how much I have changed beyond no longer yelling at my kids, I get all sappy, sentimental, and choked up.** I can't help it. And I can't help the tears either! I feel such a profound sense of amazement, joy, and gratitude that The Orange Rhino Challenge didn't just improve my relationship with my kids, but that it also improved my life overall. I know that sounds like a grandiose statement, but it's not—it's the honest to goodness truth.

As it turned out, every preventative measure and action that I fully embraced as a way to keep me from yelling became so ingrained in my behavior that I didn't just use it in situations with my kids. I also naturally started using these successful preventative measures and actions throughout the day in other situations, good or bad, my kids present or not, when I wanted to yell or didn't want to yell. I naturally started to:

Let go more.

Laugh more.

Ask for help more.

Think positively more.

Hug more.

Share my tough feelings more.

Listen more.

Enjoy my kids more.

Review my expectations more.

Forgive more.

Accept what I can't change more.

Connect with my husband more.

Do random acts of kindness more.

I started to no longer grow anger, resentment, frustration, or disappointment throughout the day, as I had done before The Orange Rhino Challenge. Instead, I started to grow more happiness, satisfaction, calm, and peace, and therefore, I started to grow a more fulfilling life. When I do the above actions, when I fully embrace these new habits that really aren't just related to not yelling but to life in general, I don't simply yell less and love my kids more—I love my life more.

Day 18: Revelations, Actions, and Tips

Orange Rhino Revelations

- **The new behaviors, attitudes, and skills I developed to help me not yell have enhanced every aspect of my life.**
- There is nothing but upside to becoming an Orange Rhino.

Today's Actions

- **Go for your goal today!** You have prepared and practiced; you have done many of the same things I did before I got my no-yelling streak under way. You are ready to go for it.

- **Get excited! Tell people about your goal, about how today is your day.** Tell your kids. Your neighbors. Your local coffee barista. Your dog. Tell everyone and anyone and get excited! Enthusiasm for goals helps people achieve them.

- **Write a plan for the day, outlining:**

  ▸ Your three favorite tips to prevent yelling both before and in the heat of the moment.

  ▸ One thing you will do for yourself to take care of you.

  ▸ Who you will text/call if needed for support.

  ▸ How you will celebrate when you achieve your goal.

_____

_____

_____

_____

_____

_____

_____

_____

_____

_____

_____

66 **Twenty years from now you will**
be more disappointed by the things
you didn't do than by the ones you did.
So throw off the bowlines. Sail away
from the safe harbor. Catch the trade winds
in your sails. Explore. Dream. Discover. **99**

—Mark Twain

Today's Tips

COOL	Dress your kids in orange, a phenomenal in-your-face reminder!
WARM	Say out loud, "You are just kids, my kids, and I love you."
HOT	Tense all muscles in the body and relax one at a time, starting with the feet and going up (I stole this from one of my son's teachers). LOVE IT!

Spontaneous tickle-fights, pile-ups-on-Mommy, hugs, kisses, and "I love yous!" are just some of the few incredible benefits of becoming an Orange Rhino.

6

Get Calm When Things (The Kids?) Are Getting Crazy

Change your thoughts and you change your world.
—Norman Vincent Peale

If I had to pick a favorite day in this challenge, it would be Day 7, the day where I learned that, nine times out of ten, my yelling wasn't because of my kids, it was because of me. Day 7, the day I remembered that the old break-up line "It's not you, it's me" is really true, especially when it comes to why I yell. My stress, my crap, my tiredness are often why I want to yell—not the kids. But what about the one time out of ten when all of my stars are aligned beautifully and I am in a really good place and yet the kids seem to know that and are legitimately trying to push every button? What about the one time out of ten when I truly feel I am parenting phenomenally and yet my kids still aren't "listening"? Still aren't "behaving"? Still are tantruming forever? You know, when kids are just being kids or just having a bad day. You know, when I don't want to be calm like an Orange Rhino but want to charge like a gray one. This chapter covers my top five go-to tools that help me change my mind-set from "Seriously, this is just ridiculous and I quit" to "Okay, I got this, I can do it."

Day 19

Let L.O.V.E. Rule:
My Thirty-Six-Year-Old Security Blanket

I am thirty-six going on thirty-seven and yes, I still have my security blanket, affectionately known as "Blankie." And yes, I still sleep with her every night. Every. Single. Night. There, I admitted it. I am a grown adult who balls up a baby blanket that is burnt in one corner, unraveling in another, missing half of its satin edge, and dons a huge hole in the middle, and then puts it under her head like a pillow. I just can't help it. You see, the thing is that she and I have been through a lot. When I was five and it was time to put my dolls down for bedtime, I took her and placed her over the Christmas candlelights in the windows because I wasn't allowed to touch the "hot candles." Well, she immediately burst into flames. Oops. Then when I was seven and I had to stop sucking my thumb (which was a total bummer), I turned to her to rub her satin edge for comfort. And then when I was twenty-nine and my husband was away on a business trip and I hated being alone in our new but old and creaking house, I curled up with her for security and comfort. What can I say but that "Blankie" is my first best friend and means a lot to me.

I know this. My husband knows this. And my boys know this, especially James, who tried so very hard to use it against me one day.

It was about 3:30 in the afternoon one record-breaking hot July day. James, who had just finished a year of half-day kindergarten (okay, more like third-day since he only went for two and a half hours), had just completed his first full day of summer camp. Up at 5:30 in the morning as always, James had already been going full speed ahead for three and a half hours before he then accrued six and a half hours of nonstop activity and uninter-rupted time away from me. As expected, I struggled through the day, missing my eldest son very, very much and worrying about how he was managing through the big physical and emotional change. And, as expected, he too struggled through the day. Scratch that. According to him, he didn't miss me at all and had a fantastic day. Good for him. His day turning upside down the minute I picked him up? Not good for him, or for us. And especially not good for Blankie.

As we pulled into the driveway after camp, his upbeat, "Yeah, I had a fun day today" quickly turned into a bawling episode of, "But I don't want to go back tomorrow. As a matter of fact, I refuse. I just want to stay home!" I parked the car and turned around, so heartbroken to see tears running from weary eyes and down a flushed, red face. Before I could even talk to him, he jumped out of the car, slammed the door, and ran into the house, screaming like mad.

I quietly got out of the car and carefully entered the house, as I kind of knew what to expect: a full-on tantrum that included throwing everything and anything at me in frustra-tion (we all know where he learned that trick, ugh, sigh!). Yup, I was spot-on. I walked in to having plastic fruit from the kid's kitchen being thrown at me. I ducked to avoid the banana only to get a pear right in the nose! Oh, did it sting. Oh, did I want to scream, "Just knock it off! Calm down already! Grow up!" But I didn't. I remained calm.

I was able to duck the next round of fruit salad and finally catch my son and hold him as he ran at me to nail me with a slice of pizza and cake. I knew the running at me was intentional; I knew it was a cry for help. Even though I truly did not appreciate having things thrown at me, I continued to remain calm, allowing me to gently hold him and say, "What is going on? Talk to me."

"It's not fair that my brothers got to leave camp early and see you before me. It's not fair that I had to be gone all day. It's just not fair!" he screamed at me, tears still streaming down his face, his body thrashing against my hug in anger. Even though my ears were ringing from his shrill voice, and I was quickly growing tired of the long tantrum, I still remained calm.

He calmed down enough to excuse himself to his room for some quiet time. He then returned, my Blankie in hand, and headed straight to the bathroom. I looked at his eyes and knew he was up to no good; rather, I knew that he wanted to do something to get my attention, to make me hold him again, to make me help him feel better about a very tough day. What better way to do that than to grab something precious to me?

"James, please give me Blankie," I said.

"No! I am going to put Blankie in the toilet," he laughed (it was an uncomfortable laugh, an "I-know-this-is-wrong-but-I-don't-know-what-to-do-with-how-crappy-and-sad-I-am-feeling" laugh).

"James, you don't want to do whatever it is you are thinking. I know you are having a rough afternoon, but don't get into trouble because of it," I said calmly.

"Too late, Mommy!" He then ran to the bathroom and dunked Blankie in the toilet. The toilet that apparently had not been flushed after someone did a #1 and a #2. Blankie now had a burnt corner *and* a corner covered in poop. Awesome.

Somehow, again, I found myself to be amazingly calm.

"James, please take Blankie out and wash her in the sink," I said as I handed him soap and turned the water on.

"Are you for real? It is covered in pee and poop," he said calmly.

"Yes, I am for real," I said steadily.

I am not sure who was more scared at this moment, my son, from intense emotions and his tantrum turned hyper tantrum turned "Mom-I-can't-believe-you-are-making-me-do-this" tantrum, or me, from my eerie calmness. I mean, I ducked the fruit and all, I slightly gasped when beloved Blankie went for a swim, but otherwise the entire episode didn't make me flinch or yell as it would have done in the past. All the episode did was push me to L.O.V.E. him more. Say what?! Yes, I loved him more because when I saw those tears fall in the car, I knew he needed my love and not my wrath. So that is just what I gave him, before, during, and after the tantrum.

I **L**istened to him share his feelings of sadness in the car, and then,

I **O**bserved his face and saw exhaustion; I observed the time of day and knew he was hungry; and I observed his sweaty face and saw an overheated little boy. After he finished washing Blankie and had calmed down a bit,

I **V**erified with him what was going on by saying to him, "James, it sounds like you are maybe a little sad and angry from being away all day. And it seems like in addition to everything, you are tired, hungry, and hot after a real long day. Am I right?" I got a very muffled, "Harumph! Yes, you are right." And then his face relaxed a bit and I could tell he was prepared to keep talking and learn, so ...

I **E**mpathized with him, sharing, "I know it feels unfair. I remember feeling sad when I had to go to school all day and couldn't stay home and play with Grandma. And I felt sad today too; I missed you big-time. Big-time. I get it. I get why you are angry. But we don't throw things or do mean things just because we are angry."

And then I got a much more relaxed little boy looking at me who said, "I know. I'm sorry I did that to Blankie. I'll pick up the toys now."

And I got a much more relaxed feeling in my own body because I had managed to stay calm when I really wanted to scream. There is nothing that triggers me more than aggressive or hyper behavior; I have no tolerance for it. But I also have no tolerance for myself when I treat aggressive behavior with aggressive behavior because it just doesn't work and makes matters worse. Love, on the other hand, love makes things better. And what have I learned really makes things better and really helps me to not yell? Love with a capital L.O.V.E.

> **Love, on the other hand, love makes things better. And what have I learned really makes things better and really helps me to not yell? Love with a capital L.O.V.E.**

When I created the L.O.V.E. acronym I figured I would use it once or twice to stay calm instead of yelling. Turns out that I use it daily, and frequently at that! Yes, when the kids are off the hook and I feel like I am caught on a hook, I stop and **L**isten to what they have to say; **O**bserve the surroundings (time, temperature, day of the week, facial expressions); **V**erify with them why they are temper tantruming, or struggling, or hyper, or who knows what; and then I **E**mpathize. I put myself in their shoes, I understand where they are coming from, why they are behaving as they are, and it helps me stay cool, calm, collected, and connected.

I guess, in many ways, L.O.V.E.ing my kids has become a new security blanket of sorts. Don't worry, Blankie, you are so not being replaced! L.O.V.E. is one of my top tools that I rely on to keep from yelling. Not only does it give me the security that I have a method to keep from yelling, but it also always comforts my kiddo and me in trying situations.

 **Day 19: Revelations, Actions, and Tips**

Orange Rhino Revelation
- When I respond to my kids with kindness, understanding, and L.O.V.E., I have a much higher chance of them hearing and embracing what I have to say, and I have a much higher chance of getting a tough situation to turn around faster.

Today's Actions
- **Let L.O.V.E. rule.**

L. isten
O. bserve
V. erify
E. mpathize

- **Practice each aspect of L.O.V.E.**
  - ▶ Be prepared that you might get the verify part wrong at first and be met with a "No, you have it all WRONG!" Stay calm and try again, perhaps asking your child to help you.
  - ▶ Be detailed when you verify and empathize, and try not to just repeat verbatim your child's words back at him/her. I learned the hard way that this can fuel the fire.
- **Make a face!** If you are struggling to understand your child, look at him/her and the facial expressions he/she is making and make the same face. This is weird but magically makes me feel what my child is feeling.
- **Love yourself!** Don't forget to love yourself as you go along on your journey: Forgive yourself and take care of yourself so that you can go forward gracefully and lovingly.

❝ Never confuse a single defeat with a final defeat. ❞

—F. Scott Fitzgerald

Today's Tips

COOL	**Orange Rhino Favorite:** Wash away growing stress. Put a warm washcloth on your face and neck and take a deep breath in, as if you were at a spa. I do this nightly at bath time; it is a go-to.
WARM	Stare at something you love in the room; finding happy moments helps erase anger.
HOT	Give a hug. Yes, this is a repeat. It just works that well and helps all parties involved!

66 **All you need is love. 99**

—John Lennon

Day 20

Find Perspective:
"At Least"—My New Favorite Mantra

Day 3, Take 2ish

Dear Perspective,

It's so nice to have breakfast with you. Whenever I start the day with you by my side, not yelling comes so much easier. I remember that kids are just kids. I remember that spilled cereal isn't the end of the world. I remember that it's more important to have a good goodbye than a rushed one. I remember that not yelling is what matters to me more than not cleaning up. Yes, Perspective, you have been a dear friend during this no-yelling challenge. You are welcome to come for breakfast, lunch, and dinner anytime. Just know that my house isn't always clean and that I am an awful cook.

Cheers,
The Orange Rhino

I remember as if it were yesterday the morning when I realized the absolute "power of perspective." The sun shone through the kitchen windows for the first time in weeks. It woke me up from my Mac-didn't-sleep-through-the-night-again stupor and calmed me down from the previous thirty minutes of brush-your-teeth and get-your-clothes-on heated discussions. Seeing the sun gave me hope that I could conquer the morning—shoot, the entire day! I put some frozen waffles in the toaster oven, took out the butter and syrup, and then just stared out the window at the beautiful winter sunrise. Yep, I was totally going to rock this day!

Well, that feeling lasted a whopping fifteenish minutes. As soon as breakfast ended and the boys headed off to play, I noticed that Mac had started crawling through syrup that had found its way to the floor. He crawled all over the kitchen floor, leaving not-so-cute, sticky, messy knee marks everywhere. EVERYWHERE. My sleep-deprived self just wanted to scream. But I didn't. I don't know what came over me at that moment (maybe the sun did give me strength?), but instead of screaming at Mac and Andrew, the reason the syrup had found its way to the floor in the first place, I just smiled. It was all good.

It was JUST syrup.

After five and a half years of parenting and several years of yelling over small stuff like syrup, I finally found perspective and it has stuck to me ever since. After I cleaned up the kitchen, I quickly jotted down the "Dear Perspective" letter above, followed by:

Perspective. That's all I need. Eight out of ten times I'm yelling for no real good reason at all. For example, the fact that Andrew is learning to feed himself is more important than the fact that Mac just crawled in the syrup that dripped off the piece of waffle that fell on the table after it fell off the fork.

I couldn't finish the middle of the post because, you know, that's life with kids, and I couldn't write it that night because, you know, that's life when you have young kids and you fall asleep at 8:00, but I did manage to squeeze out an ending:

Somehow I made it through today without yelling. And trust me, today the odds were stacked against me. But I did it. And I think it is all because of Perspective. I stopped and looked at things differently, and that made all the difference.

Perspective. That's all I need. Eight out of ten times I'm yelling for no real good reason at all.

Yes, I am certain perspective did save the day because it regularly does for me ever since I discovered its power. And I have two small words to thank for helping me find perspective when I desperately need it ...

At least.

Two small words that can make a huge difference, so much so that they are my new favorite words—well, after L.O.V.E. Seriously. I started adding these two words to any moment when I want to yell over something smallish and, *voilà*, life seems easier because it is filled with newfound perspective that things could be worse.

"Oh, there is syrup dripping on the floor. AT LEAST the entire bottle isn't dripping."

"Oh, he is climbing on the table. AT LEAST he isn't hanging by the chandelier."

"Oh, he destroyed his bedroom. AT LEAST his brothers didn't copy him."

"Oh, my life is so crazy with three kids with different therapy needs. AT LEAST they are in my life to love."

I could go on and on and on. I think I will, at least for a bit.

"Ugh. I have 363 days left of this challenge ... hey, AT LEAST I have gone 2 days, which is better than none."

"Ugh. I yelled today ... hey, AT LEAST I am trying to not yell."

See, "at least" really works wonders. Does "at least" not suit your fancy? Substitute any other word or phrase that helps you see the situation in a positive light. My other popular choice? "I'm grateful."

"It seems I have so many triggers ... hey, I'M GRATEFUL that I know who I am and what I need to work on."

No matter which words you choose, the power of perspective remains the same. Is it always easy to find perspective when things are rough? Is it always easy to stop and say "at least" or "I'm grateful" and keep on going? No, it isn't. Sometimes the moment is too frustrating to be able to find perspective, to even want to find perspective. Sometimes it takes me longer to find perspective than I wish. Sometimes it takes three seconds, sometimes three hours, and other more difficult times it can take three days or even three months. But when I finally find that perspective, I truly feel a weight lifted. Do I care that it took me that long to get to that moment, or that it was hard to get there? Nope. Because AT LEAST I got there!

66 If you don't like something,
change it.
If you can't change it,
change your attitude. **99**

—Maya Angelou

LEGOs on the floor are a huge trigger— I hate stepping on them! That said, this scene made my skin crawl, until I thought, "Hey, at least James dumped all of them in one-ish spot; at least he is wonderfully engrossed in a creative activity; and at least the colorful 'mess' is from LEGOs and not permanent markers!

Orange Rhino Revelation

• Perspective is a powerful tool to keep me from yelling.

Today's Actions

• **Use the "at least" technique throughout the day to defuse your desire to yell.** If this phrase doesn't work for you, find a saying that does work.

• **Try using it to also defuse your child's tantrum,** as in, "Mommy, there is a green thing on my pizza." My reply: "Well, at least it's just part of the sauce and not a green booger. That would be gross!" Be creative, be outrageous, be funny. The more outrageous you are, the better! My kids have learned the "at least" technique and have managed their own disappointments themselves. It is that simple and powerful to do!

• **Gain perspective of how well you are doing on this challenge.** Write down three areas where you have seen improvement in your life since you started your Orange Rhino Challenge, noting that even if you aren't where you want to be yet, AT LEAST you have taken the step and are on the right path!

_____

_____

_____

_____

_____

_____

_____

_____

66 Life isn't about waiting for the
storm to pass ... It's about
learning to dance in the rain! **99**

—Vivian Greene

Today's Tips

COOL	Do absolutely nothing for one minute (longer, if time allows!) but watch your kids; this always fills me up with a little more love and a lot of perspective about what really matters.
WARM	Put the television on for longer than normally feels okay in really tough moments; I find a little extra TV isn't the end of the world when I am at the end of my rope.
HOT	Whistle. Loudly. This forces me to focus on my breathing (which I can't stand!) and eventually annoys my kids so they redirect attention at me.

Day 21

Laugh When You Just Want to Scream: The Great Toothpick Debacle of 2013

I always get my best sleep on vacation with my kids ... NOT! As in not ever, not a chance, not likely, and sleep is just not gonna happen. My kids go to bed later, wake up earlier, and in between toss and turn and wake up numerous times either from excitement of being in a new place or from fear of being in the dark in a new place. They don't get good sleep, I don't get good sleep; they get more hyper and I get obviously happier. Again, NOT. Those first few mornings on vacation when they are up earlier and I am sleep deprived, I am cranky for a good two hours until we start the fun plans of the day and I remember that the loss of sleep is totally worth it. That said, I now expect these mornings to stink, so they don't bother me as much. I find my coffee, followed by my empathy and perspective, and yelling doesn't find me.

My mother, however, well, she just ain't used to the wicked early in the morning vacation we're-so-excited-we're-bouncing-off-the-walls shenanigans. At all.

I will never forget August 18, 2013. It was just too hysterical. I mean, the morning was so wacked that I couldn't make this up. Shoot, I can't even type right now because I am laughing just thinking about it.

Anywho, around 6:00 a.m. I finally let the boys out of the guest bedroom at my parent's house to go downstairs. They ran down the stairs and pulled out Grandma's stash of LEGOs and began building as I drank my coffee. Not two seconds later Riley, the largest, loudest, most rambunctious Kerry Blue Terrier ever, ran out of Grandma's room so excited to see the boys and jumped into the middle of the LEGO bucket spilling them EVERYWHERE. LEGOs flew through the air as tears fell down faces of little LEGO Builders. Edward was so mad that he immediately grabbed Riley's collar and opened a door to put him outside. It was a great plan—it just wasn't well executed! (I blame his pure exhaustion and frustration!) Anyhow, instead of opening the door that led to the closed-in backyard, he opened the door to the garage. Andrew had followed Edward and clearly thinking he was helping him execute the grand plan to remove Riley, he opened the garage for Riley setting him free into the huge, ungated community park!

Riley tore off, barking and waking everyone up, including Grandma. Stellar, boys, stellar. Grandma came out of her room in her nightgown, her hair sticking up and her eyes half closed.

"What is that racket? Where is Riley?" she barked.

"Oh, Mom, it's Riley. He got out kind of on purpose, kind of by accident. I tried to get him but he won't come in," I said, equally as half asleep.

"Boys, you clean up those LEGOs right now while I get Riley," she said, her bark a little softer.

"Okay, Grandma." They finished the cleanup easily, as they had already begun per my instructions. Riley, of course, ran in toward them again but got corralled into a bedroom, so as to avoid another LEGO explosion. The boys were now all riled up from the dog escaping and watching Grandma and me run around like crazy ladies trying to catch her, so I tried to settle them down with a quiet, focused activity.

They seemed content and calmish working on a puzzle, so I thought it was safe to run to the bathroom. I was sorely mistaken. While I was in the bathroom for a whopping, (what, thirty seconds, maybe sixty?) my boys had abandoned the puzzle after spotting Grandpa's (and also their) favorite gadget: a toothpick holder that looks like a bird. When you press down the beak, out comes a toothpick. And, as I quickly learned, when you press it over and over and over again (because that is obviously really fun and cool) out come a lot of toothpicks!

The second I stepped out of the bathroom I yelped, "Ouch!"

"What did I just step on?" I asked firmly. I looked down to see that my parents' brand new carpet now had about thirty toothpicks standing up in it.

"What is this?" I said. "That is your grandfather's. Put it back now!" I stated, more firmly than before.

"But Mommy, we are setting a trap for Riley so if he goes for the door again he will step on the toothpicks," they said innocently. I had to admit, it was kind of an ingenious plan and that quieted my growing yell.

"A+ for creativity and design boys, but not so much on using something without asking. Clean up now, please," I said. Meanwhile, Grandma had walked into the bathroom from the other direction, completely unaware of the great Toothpick Trap that awaited her on the other side. Well, when she came out and stepped on one of the not-yet-picked-up toothpicks, she started to scream.

"BOYS! What is ...." She was quickly interrupted by a "BEEP. BEEP. BEEP. BEEP," at a decibel so painful we all wanted to scream. Edward and Andrew covered their ears as I ran to find James and Mac, thinking it was the fire alarm and that we needed to get out immediately. James popped his head from around the corner, scared as can be from the noise. But Mac, Mac had disappeared in the two minutes that transpired during the toothpick debacle. I ran upstairs and found him sitting in a corner by a carbon monoxide plug-in machine. He was frozen with fear.

"Button," he said over and over and over. Yes, he had pressed a button on the detector and set it off. I quickly tried to stop the noise, because if I didn't want to yell before, I was there now. Like, really there. Like "are you f*ing kidding me" there. I had no luck. I couldn't turn it off.

Then the phone rang.

"Hello? This is your security provider. Is there a fire?" someone asked.

"No!" My mom said. "My two-year-old grandson pressed a button. How do we turn it off? The noise is making all the boys scared and they are crying and screaming. We need it off now!"

"You need to press the code into your alarm system," she told my mom.

"Well, sh*t," she said, "I don't know the code and my husband is on the West Coast. It isn't even 4 a.m. there. He won't wake up. Isn't there another way?"

Yelling won't accomplish a thing; it will just get you all riled up. Just laugh.

"No. You need the code or the firemen will have to come."

My mom tried and tried my dad. No answer. I punched in all the codes that my dad had used when we were kids. Nothing bloody worked, and now the kids were hysterical. Until, knock. Knock.

"Grandma, there are four firemen at the door," James said, totally psyched.

The minute they stepped foot in the house, of course, the alarm stopped. I had done it! I totally felt like Superwoman at the moment, albeit I was five minutes late in my arrival. The guys gave the kids high fives and let them see the fire truck. All was good. My mom and I had had three minutes of calm, and it felt as though we could conquer the day.

Until …

We all came in the house from seeing the truck, and James and Edward were so excited that they threw their lovies into the air … into the chandelier that hung so high only a ladder could reach it. *"Seriously? Are you kidding me? After everything already this morning and it's not even 7? Now I needed to get a ladder out? Not happening,"* I thought to myself, breathing through my nose so I wouldn't yell, my nostrils flaring like my son's favorite dragon toy. Oh, I so wanted to spit fire!

Grandma, well, she struggled to not yell a lot more than I did. She started to yell and I put my hand on her arm and said, "Mom, sometimes you just have to laugh. Go ahead. Laugh. What else can you do in this moment? Yelling won't accomplish a thing; it will just get you all riled up. Just laugh. Besides, you have to admit, all of this is kind of funny! Go on, just laugh already! You had better practice chilling out because this week of 'vacation' is gonna be crazy!"

And she laughed. And I laughed. And it felt awesome, so much better than yelling! Laughing calmed both of us down and enabled me to inform James and Edward calmly (therefore clearly and in a manner that could be understood) that the lovies would stay where they landed for the day because they knew the rule about throwing things toward the chandelier.

I went to bed with a huge smile on my face that night. I just couldn't help it. The day had been totally out of control and crazy at times, but totally incredible too, because I chose laughter instead of losing it.

Orange Rhino Revelations

- Laughter really helps defuse a yell and puts things in perspective.

- Expecting, accepting, and therefore embracing that my life is crazy instead of trying to fight it, trying to change it, gives me a lot more energy and patience to not yell in crazy situations.

- "Craziness is an acceptable part of life at all times." My son's teacher wrote this to me when I emailed her, "I am so sorry for changing the date of our meeting again and for all the craziness." Um, can I get a HECK YEAH for this piece of brilliance?!

Today's Actions

- **Laugh when you just want to scream.** Fake it if you need to. The old advice "Smile if you are cranky and you'll feel happier" applies to laughing too.

- **Join the craziness—you might just find that it is fun.** Set up a toothpick fort. Skip with your kids. Throw things high in the air to see if they will get stuck. Tell funny stories with your children, have them tell funny stories. Make a funny, backward meal. Do something absolutely outrageous (maybe have them dress you up in their clothes?); just have fun with your kids! This always helps me chill out and be in a better place to not yell. Plus, the extra connection time with my boys increases their willingness to listen to me when necessary.

66 It is impossible for you to be angry
and laugh at the same time.
Anger and laughter are mutually exclusive
and you have the power to choose either. **99**

—Wayne Dyer

Today's Tips

COOL	Take a deep breath, or two or three. If you are deep breathing, you can't yell!
WARM	Tickle the child you want to yell at. Laughter does the body good, more so than milk, I think.
	Tell your children, "Nose to knee!" This works phenomenally well in the car as a good, fun distraction.
HOT	Bang your fists on your chest like a gorilla. Try your hardest to not laugh when you start feeling absolutely ridiculous. Better yet, try this in public.

❝ A day without laughter is a day wasted. ❞

—Charlie Chaplin

Day 22

Tell Yourself Yelling Doesn't Work:
... And I Dropped to My Knees and Cried

I wrote the following just weeks into my Orange Rhino Challenge during the phase where I had already gone ten days not yelling and was struggling to stay on track. I never shared it because I didn't have the courage. I didn't yet feel prepared to be so vulnerable, and I didn't want my harsh realization that my yelling problem had greatly affected my children to become real. And, well, sharing it publicly would make it extremely real. So instead, I hid this post and never looked back at the pain. Until now. The good news is that looking back now doesn't cause pain, but relief and joy that I have changed.

February 3, 2012

This morning Andrew accidentally bumped James's LEGO creation, the creation that was perfectly symmetrical, the creation that was perfectly planned, and the creation that was perfectly keeping James focused and happy. James immediately exploded and jumped up from his spot on the floor next to me, ready to go after Andrew. Instead, he accidentally got me. I got caught in the explosion and got nailed in the face with an elbow. It hurt. I too immediately exploded and jumped up and started screaming, "What is your problem today? Why can't you just chill out?" I took one look at James, his tears, and his broken LEGO creation and pulled it together. I dropped to my knees next to James who lay crumpled on the floor, and went to hold him.

And he just collapsed into my arms. And I held him.
And I rocked him.
And for the first time ever, I cried with him.

*I cried for him. I cried for me. I cried for both of us because I knew both of us were hurting from the arrival of his new meltdowns. James hugged me back and just let me hold him and love him. It's been a long while since he let me do that— hold him, that is. And it's been a long while since I've done that—hold him, that is. I haven't held him really in ages because, sadly, I have been too busy feeling angry and frustrated with him and his newly developed major meltdowns to stop and hold him. Who am I kidding, **I've been too busy yelling at him, putting him down in order to try to shame him into getting it together, to be able to see that what he needed was to be picked up and loved.***

Let me tell you, stopping and loving him and feeling his pain was a lot more rewarding than yelling at him and causing him more pain. At that moment, while he rubbed my back and I rubbed his, as he cried on my shoulder and I cried on his, I felt a connection as deep as the first time I held him. I just wanted to hold him forever. I just wanted to tell him that I promise, it will be all right, that the meltdowns will just melt away with time.

> Let me tell you, stopping and loving him and feeling his pain was a lot more rewarding than yelling at him and causing him more pain.

You see, James, like me, has some sensory challenges. He shares my sensitivity to sound, touch, smell, and taste. We have just identified this and it breaks my heart. It breaks my heart because I fear that he will have the same difficult and long path that I did as I began to understand and manage my own sensory challenges. It breaks my heart because while I know many of the joys he'll feel as a "sensational" child, like the overwhelming joy of smelling the ocean and the overwhelming peace of hearing the ocean, I also know of the many struggles he'll face, like not throwing food when it tastes mushy, not pulling his hair out when it is too hot, not yelling when massively overwhelmed by the physical environment. And it breaks my heart because I feel, somehow, that it is my fault and I just want to scream right now, "Damn you DNA! Why did you have to pass down my weakness to a sweet little boy?! Why couldn't you just have given him the good stuff? The good qualities? Why did you have to set him up to struggle like me?!"

But right now, it's not just the news that James has some sensory challenges like me that I am mad at; I am also mad at myself. I am mad at myself that for years I have yelled at James for behavior that he was trying so hard to control but couldn't because he didn't yet have the tools, because we didn't yet have the awareness that he needed more guidance. I yelled at him for screaming at me, for crying endlessly because he was hot. I yelled at him for refusing to try new foods because the smells made him want to throw up. I yelled at him for starting fights with his younger brothers because they were sitting too close to him. I yelled nasty things like, "Why can't you just get it together?" only to hear him sob back, "Nothing, Mom. I'm not trying to be a bad kid. I'm really not, I'm just having a hard time with all the noise and it makes me go nuts. I need quiet."

Ouch.

Oh, oh, how I used to yell at him a lot and not hear what he told me he needed. I just yelled, thinking that it would work, that it would stop the insanity. Or as the case would be, I guess I wasn't thinking. **Because if I were, I would have seen that yelling didn't work, that it never, ever stopped the tough moment but just made it tougher.** All yelling did was make James cry louder and longer because the intensity of my yell didn't just hurt his feelings, but it put his already fried senses under further attack.

Yelling at James literally made things worse. Holding him, listening to him, acknowledging his feelings, that, THAT made things better. Way better.

> Yelling at James literally made things worse. Holding him, listening to him, acknowledging his feelings, that, THAT made things better. Way better. Instantly better.

Instantly better. I feel less anger toward him, less frustration, and I know he feels that way toward me. And I feel less anger toward myself, less frustration. I just feel more hope that I now have a clue how to better help him. This is such a relief because James has such a beautiful soul. I need to nourish it, embrace, and not destroy it.

*I know my yelling at him was slowly destroying his caring heart, and I will not let that happen. I simply will not. **I will not let my anger squelch the love he so openly shares with the world and me.** I will not let my anger squelch his huge, sensitive, empathetic heart, the heart that says, "Mommy, it must be hard having four kids." The heart that says, "Mommy, I hear sirens, I hope everyone is okay." The heart that said to me when we finally stopped hugging earlier, "Mommy, I love you. Thank you for stopping yelling at me."*

You are welcome, James. You are welcome. I promise it will be all right. It will. It really, really will; I mean it and I believe it.

That day helped get me back on track. I haven't yelled at James since, and it feels so fantastic. James is doing great, which is of no surprise. He has his sensory stuff under control (for the most part) and is just focusing on being a sensational child, and this time I am not talking about the senses, but just about being outright awesome.

Orange Rhino Revelations

- Yelling doesn't work. **Except in emergencies.** Period.

- When people yell at me, I can't understand what is being requested, so how can I do what is asked, especially if I have lost all desire to respond?

- The same goes for my kids. They can't hear me when I am screaming. If I want to teach them, I need to speak quietly and in a way that they are open to hearing what I have to say.

- The more I yelled, the more I was tuned out. By not yelling, except when I really need to (such as in emergencies), my yell matters big-time and works more effectively. (In those cases, a clear, concise, simple STOP or DANGER does the job.)

- Yelling seemed like it worked at first because it scared my kids into stopping a certain behavior, but based on how many times the behavior resurfaced, it is clear that it didn't work because it didn't teach my children to stop doing the behavior in the long run.

Today's Actions

- **Tell yourself that yelling doesn't work.**

- **Ask yourself, "What happens when my kids yell at me to do something?"**
  Does it make me want to help them? Does it inspire me to be kind or angry? Does it work? Does it make things better or worse? Take these answers and embrace them, knowing that your kids would probably respond the same way. Heck, why don't you ask them?

- **Now ask yourself, "What happens when I yell at my kids to do something?"**

  - ▸ Is it really working as effectively as you want?

  - ▸ If they respond immediately, why? Is it fear? Is it perhaps because they are trained to wait until you yell to respond?

- **If you feel yelling is the only way to get your kids to listen, brainstorm three alternatives now.** Mine would be (1) walk over to them and get down eye to eye, (2) make physical contact as I speak, and (3) ask them to repeat back to me what I said.

- **Turn the mirror on yourself (hard, I know) and ask yourself, "Have I been clear in my expectations? Did I ask in a manner that my kids can hear me?"** I am so guilty of asking them to do something when they are in the middle of playing a game and are at a distance. Two strikes against me: I am not close and demanding attention, and they are involved and will strug gle to focus. I need to get them to stop before they will listen.

❝ Kind words can be short and easy
to speak, but their echoes are truly endless. ❞

—Mother Theresa

Today's Tips

COOL ☺	Drink out of an orange straw throughout the day as a simple reminder of the color orange, of warmth. Added bonus: Drinking more water throughout the day will help you mentally feel better.
WARM ☺	Start doing "crab walks" to entertain your kids and to release those good chemicals that come from exercise. For added fun, do a crab walk race with everyone. Your kids will kick your butt, you will fall on yours, and you'll forget all about yelling. (Crab walk looks like the opposite of a push-up. Put your hands under you, bend your knees, and go!)
HOT ☹	Yell into a kitchen cabinet in desperate times; cereal boxes don't have feelings, kids do.

Day 23

Talk Out Loud:
"Mommy Is Scared"

For much of my childhood, I felt teased for being too emotional, for crying too much, for overreacting too much, for taking things too personally. And so, for much of my young adulthood and certainly into adulthood as I met new friends, my husband included, I tried to make sure that I wasn't "too much" because the pain of being teased still felt very real and very raw. I held a lot of my real feelings deep inside so that I wouldn't come across as having too much baggage, so that I wouldn't turn people off "too much" and therefore have too hard a time making and keeping friends.

I became an expert at not showing my emotions (okay, more like a cold robot). I would show emotional support to others, but I tried my hardest not to let on how I really felt. I tried my hardest to keep all my feelings bottled up, close to my heart where no one could access them and make fun of me for being "too much." My plan worked really well until I became a mom and I experienced so many amazingly powerful moments that I couldn't hide my joy, pride, and love. I just felt the strong urge to gush and share how I felt about my children, so I did. I just made sure it was only to my husband and to my children.

But I still made sure to keep the other emotions, the more "dark" ones, to myself for fear of being judged "too much." This plan kept working really well until I became an Orange Rhino and realized that keeping in all my fears, frustrations, and disappointments about my children, and keeping in all my fears, frustrations, and sorrows about my life, well, it did me no good. It turned out that holding back my emotions just because I feared being "too much," totally backfired. **By not letting my emotions out, it just made all my negative emotions build and build and build to the point where they came out in way, way "too much" yelling.**

So holding my emotions in no longer existed as an option for me if I wanted to keep on being an Orange Rhino. I forced myself to start talking again, to start getting back to the old me, the real me. I started slowly by sharing with myself more, by letting myself feel again, cry again, and then I started sharing with my friends more, with my family more. And I started sharing with The Orange Rhino community, and wouldn't you know, it felt great. It felt great to be me again, to not be hiding anything. It felt great to not be afraid; it felt great to no longer hold all the tension and anxiety inside. And, it felt great that not yelling became so much easier as a result of my opening up.

As I gained confidence in the power of sharing my feelings and as I gained a deeper understanding of how it helped me to not yell, I couldn't help but think of my boys and all the times they hit, kicked, screamed, bit, punched, pinched, spit, and all the other ways they showed frustration and anger. I couldn't help but think of how I always replied to those situations with, "Use your words, not your hands. Tell me what is going on." I couldn't help but think that they struggled to use their words not only because they were kids and didn't know how, but also because I hadn't shown them how to use their words. I had just shown them how to keep their feelings to themselves and then act out when it became too much.

So I started sharing my feelings with them, as appropriate. I wanted my boys to learn that sharing emotions is not only an okay thing to do, but also an important thing to do, a necessary thing to do. **And I wanted them to learn that talking about feelings and labeling them is a great alternative to yelling.** Fortunately—or unfortunately, depending on how you look at it—I have had a lot of big opportunities to demonstrate this lesson during my journey.

When Mac was barely fourteen months, he had his first seizure. A few nights after Thanksgiving, he had his third and worst seizure ever. After racing to the emergency room to give him oxygen, all I remember hearing from the doctor was, "Neurologist. Pronto. Epilepsy or brain tumor. Go tomorrow." So "go tomorrow" we did. The neurology appointment wasn't bad, but it wasn't good either. The doctor confirmed that we did need to rule out a brain tumor as the source of the seizures and that we needed to run a three-day in-hospital test stat to also rule out temporal lobe epilepsy. Based on the video I had taken during his seizure (don't ask me how I thought to do that under the circumstances), he did feel strongly that it was most likely epilepsy and not a tumor, but still, still I left the office scared beyond scared.

Sharing my feelings instead of keeping them inside made me feel calmer and more connected to my sons during a difficult week, and importantly, it kept me from screaming unnecessarily.

So much so that when I walked in the door to the house and got bombarded by my nervous boys, I didn't feel like being a parent. I didn't feel like being responsible. I just wanted to cry. And cry. And cry. I wanted to feel scared and sad. I didn't feel like dealing with all the energy that my boys had at that moment, all the excitement they had to see me after a long day away, all the fear they felt about Mac. And yet, I wanted to be there for them at the same time. I wanted to hug them and love them and feel the goodness that was real in front of me at that moment. I was so conflicted with emotions: wanting to hide, but wanting to be present. And that overwhelming confusion actually made me want to scream at them to stop running around and to stop jumping on me.

So I did what I knew I had to do, what The Orange Rhino Challenge had forced me to start doing again: I talked about my feelings and I told them what Mommy was experiencing.

"Hi, guys. I am excited to see you, too. I love you so much. Listen. Here's the thing. Mommy has had a long day with the baby. I've missed you tons but Mommy is tired and feeling a little stressed and scared. So I need you to help me. I need you to play loudly in the basement or quietly up here. I get cranky when I am stressed and I don't want to get cranky with you. I want to love you lots. Can you help me?"

It worked. Sharing my feelings instead of keeping them inside made me feel calmer and more connected to my sons during a difficult week, and more importantly, it kept me from screaming unnecessarily. Sharing my feelings worked that day I went to the neurologist, and has worked many other days since. You know what else works? Crying. I cried that morning with my boys when they expressed their anger that Mac was getting all my attention lately because of the seizures. I just couldn't help it. And you know what? I was okay with that and I still am because if I want to truly show my boys how to manage emotions, I need to let myself express all of them, even the ugly, uncomfortable ones, in front of them. Yes, I filter what I share to adjust to an age-appropriate level, but I still push myself to tell them how I feel instead of yelling at them so that they can learn to do the same when angry.

Sometimes I still fall back on my own fears and worry that I share "too much" with everyone in my life. But then I think of all the times that sharing has kept me from screaming, all the times that I have heard my boys share instead of act out, and all I can think is, it might be "too much" but it is helping all of us stay calmer and more in control and there is no such thing as "too much" time spent not yelling.

Day 23: Revelations, Actions, and Tips

Orange Rhino Revelations

- Bottled-up emotions do me no good; I must share how I feel if I don't want to yell.

- Labeling my emotions instead of yelling encourages my kids to feel empathy when I am upset/sad/stressed; it also teaches them how to label and manage their own emotions (which leads to a lot fewer tantrums!).

- There is no shame, just courage, in feeling emotions and sharing them.

Today's Actions

- **Talk out loud, share your emotions out loud.** Practice sharing all emotions, bad and good. Say when you are happy, ecstatic, proud, full of love. Say when you are tired, hungry, stressed. Say when you are angry, sad, or worried. Especially say the emotions when you want to yell. Say them, don't scream them.

  - ▶ If you feel angry toward a child, be sure to use "I" statements and focus on the behavior and not the child, because that will backfire. "I am angry that the toys are still on the floor" instead of "I am angry at you for not picking up the toys."

  - ▶ If you struggle at first to talk out loud, write your feelings down and then if you can, read them to someone. This is an especially good exercise to do if you are feeling frustrated with your progress to Yell Less and Love More.

- **Play charades with your kids.** On a good day, when all the stars are aligned, practice teaching each other emotions by playing charades. No formal game necessary; just have kids make faces and you guess what they feel. Then you do the same.

- **Have your kids draw emotions.** If your children are too young to grasp talking, when they are angry give them a pen and paper and have them draw how they feel. This is a BIG one in our house. Sometimes they just scribble angrily, but that seems to release some of the anger, too. It even works for adults. Just sayin'.

❝ Don't worry that children never listen to you; worry that they are always watching you. **❞**

—Robert Fulghum

Today's Tips

COOL	**Orange Rhino Favorite:** Eat a carrot or an apple, just make sure it is something crunchy and hard, so you can crunch stress away.
WARM	Pop some orange M&Ms into your mouth; chocolate is a great mood changer.
HOT	Cry. Yup. Cry. Show your child you are frustrated. This often brings empathy and new behavior, and it will probably make you feel better.

7

Find Warmth When All You Feel Is Anger

" Speak when you are angry and you will make the best speech you will ever regret. **"**

—Ambrose Bierce

Look deeply at the name "Orange Rhino." Do you see the hidden word in there? Here's a hint: I didn't see it when I first created my moniker, which is rather ironic because it is one of the main emotions I feel right before I yell. Do you see it yet? What about now: orANGERhino. Crazy, right?! Yes, anger is hidden inside my moniker, which is unreal because so much of my Orange Rhino journey was about uncovering the hidden triggers and personal issues that caused my anger, and uncovering how I could personally find warmth when all I felt was said anger. This chapter shares my top five go-to ways to help me find warmth so that that I don't make the best speech I will ever regret at my boys. Before you get started reading, though, here's an acronym I created to help me remember when it is time to start seeking warmth; hopefully, you will find it as useful as well.

A.N.G.E.R. stands for:

Annoyed

Negative thoughts

Grumpy attitude (physical signs of a yell start)

Exasperated feelings

Rageful, regretful yell!

I use the above as a scale to keep my attitude in check. When I am annoyed and I don't change my attitude, I get to level N and get all negative. If I don't get my attitude in check then, I get full-on grumpy. I know that if I get to level G, grumpy, that I need to immediately start seeking warmth or else I will head quickly into the exasperated and rageful levels. Here's to keeping things G-rated and to having some of the best moments you will never forget!

Day 24

Reminisce about What Happens When You Don't Yell: "Mommy, Will You Love Me in Heaven?"

A mere 107 days into my no more yelling journey I had the most amazing, gosh-I-am-so-beyond-grateful-that-I-started-the-Orange-Rhino-Challenge moment ever. That 107th night, I shared the following story on my blog:

> As I have written before, as much as I love my kids, by the time bedtime rolls around, I am done. I am ready to tuck everyone in, give each boy one last kiss and snuggle, and then shut all the doors and go downstairs to relax. After 7:15 p.m., if I hear footsteps sneaking out, this mama gets pissed. Unfortunately (or fortunately?), I can't get pissed anymore because of The Orange Rhino Challenge. I can't yell and carry on like I am accustomed to doing in such situations. Tonight I was challenged to not yell. Oh, was I challenged. And tonight I kept my promise. And oh, did it make me cry.
>
> I had just settled down on the couch with a nice glass of wine. I was not ten seconds into a deep thought of, "Oh, this is nice. It is so quiet," when I heard footsteps slowly making their way down the hall toward the stairs. I knew immediately whom they belonged to. James. Dear, sweet, James who loves to sneak out and try to convince us that he needs one more cracker, a sip of ice cold water, or better yet, five minutes of playing Angry Birds on my husband's iPad in order to fall asleep. AS IF.
>
> I ever so gently placed my wine glass down, being rather deliberate in the gentleness because what I really wanted to do was throw the glass in the fireplace. I was that annoyed. Let's just say it has been a looooong week. This mama is beyond done. Between baby showers, birthday parties, school parties, doctors' appointments, and unanticipated speech evaluations for two more boys, I just needed some time to decompress tonight. I had no desire to play the cracker/water/iPad/I need to pee/one more book game. My patience tank was empty. My empathy tank was empty. The only thing full was my wine glass, and clearly that wasn't going to be empty soon. I found whatever self-control I could muster and headed toward the stairs.
>
> James knew I was coming; I'm pretty sure my stomping feet up the stairs gave it away. The soft footsteps I heard moments before turned into a mad dash for his room. All his attempts to not be busted went out the window when he accidentally SLAMMED his door shut. I was pissed before, but now I was REALLY pissed because I was certain the loud bang would wake his brothers. I grabbed the doorknob and somewhat aggressively opened the door to his room. I wanted to scream, "Get back in BED! NOW!"

But before I could even open my mouth, I took one look at his face. He had the look that said, "Mommy, don't yell at me. Something is wrong and that's why I can't fall asleep."

I walked over to his bed, taking deep, agitated breaths that were so loud they could wake his brothers. I was still fuming, but my son's voice defused the desire to yell.

Just as I was about to start in with my bedtime lecture, James's shy, concerned, and quavering voice began. "Mommy, will you love me even when I go to heaven?" (Um, holy sh*t, I wasn't prepared for that.)

Tears in my eyes, then, and now, "Yes, of course. I will always love you."

"But Mommy, will you love me even when you are in heaven?"

"Yes, of course. I will always, always love you. Forever and ever."

"Because you have a big heart, Mommy???"

"Yes, and because I love you tons and tons. I will never stop loving you."

"Okay. I love you, Mommy."

"I love you, too."

He then rolled over, closed his eyes, and settled in to sleep. Hearing "I love you, too," was all he needed to hear to fall asleep.

I tucked him in again and gave him another kiss and another hug, a hug that I didn't want to end. I wanted to hold on to that moment forever. I wanted to hold on to James forever, for him to feel just how much I love him, for him to feel at ease, for me to feel at ease. The mere thought of him ever being in heaven before me breaks my heart. The mere thought of him even worrying about that breaks my heart.

I cried leaving the room. I cried because of the innocence of the conversation. I cried because of the fear that the conversation could be true someday. I cried because I love him so much. And I cried because I was so glad that I had that conversation, and that I hadn't yelled.

All James needed was for me to listen to him and to hear me say "I love you" one more time. I can't imagine how tonight would have gone down if when I opened that door I had started screaming like I used to. Oh wait, yes I can. He would have started bawling. It would have taken thirty minutes to calm him down. And then he would have fallen asleep upset and still worrying about whether or not I would love him forever. Instead of that, we shared a truly beautiful moment.

So yes, not yelling is worth it. Because in not yelling, I shared this moment with my son. And I don't think I will ever forget it. Ever.

> I realized in that moment that I had no idea how many remarkable moments and conversations like that one had been missed because I had been too busy yelling.

And I haven't. It's impossible to forget this story, not just because of its beauty, but also because it has had such a profound impact on my life. After I stopped crying that night and I settled myself into my couch again, I started crying some more, this time more intensely. I realized in that moment that I had no idea how many remarkable moments and conversations like that one had been missed because I had been too busy yelling. How many times did my kids just need to hear "I love you" one more time and instead I yelled, "BE QUIET"? How many times were my kids worried about life and needed to ask me questions to find security and I just yelled, "ENOUGH! I NEED A BREAK"? How many times do my kids need me to reassure them, to share in their joy over an achievement, to fuel their confidence, and instead they didn't get me, but some Gray Charging Rhino type of mom with no compassion, patience, or warmth? I didn't need to count. I knew the answer was "a lot more than I care to count."

At the time, this realization made me quite, quite sad. But since, it has made me quite, quite happy. I often recall this story to push me to find warmth for my children when I feel anger, frustration, and shortness. **I push myself to remember that good things can happen when I don't yell.** And I push myself to remember that good things might not, but they most definitely will not, happen if I yell. As a result of my not yelling, I have been surprised numerous times with spontaneous "Mommy, I just wanted to say I love you." In fact, I have heard that so many times when I otherwise would have yelled that I can't count.

As I wrote on my blog on my 107th day, "Not yelling is hard. WICKED, wicked hard at times. But yes, it is so worth it." Oh, is it ever.

Day 24: Revelations, Actions, and Tips

Orange Rhino Revelations

- Don't assume that your kids are up to no good; they might be, but they also might not be.

- My boys might be young, but they still can have mature and profound thoughts. If I listen to them first (especially their explanations) instead of making assumptions and reacting with a yell, we often can progress forward peacefully.

- Not yelling has made my life richer because I am now having so many poignant conversations with my kids that I previously would have shut down.

Today's Actions

- **Remember a time during this journey when you wanted to yell but didn't.**
  Write about it in the space below, focusing on how good you felt. Tell this story often to yourself and your support network so it becomes ingrained in your head and ready for retrieval when you need support to not yell.

  _____

  _____

  _____

  _____

  _____

  _____

- **Ask your child these two questions. Commit to memory the answers** to the second question and call on that response when you want to yell.

  - ▸ How does it feel when I yell?
  - ▸ How does it feel when I don't yell?

- **When, not if, you catch yourself before yelling today, do a fist pump.** Or something celebratory. Seriously. Let yourself feel proud and know that that feeling is just one of many good things that happen when you don't yell.

66 Man cannot discover new oceans
unless he has the courage to
leave sight of the shore. 99

—Andre Gide

Today's Tips

COOL	Share stories of when you were a kid and got excited; showing my kids that I too was once a kid is a great connector and mood changer.
WARM	Try to do a somersault; this always makes me laugh because I just can't do it anymore!
HOT	Stomp your feet like a gray rhino but know that you are becoming an Orange Rhino in that moment by choosing to stomp out the yell.

Day 25

Remember, Kids Are People Too:
If I Were a Kid ...

"Mommy, what time do you go to bed?" Edward asked me ever so sweetly as I cuddled up next to him on his bed. By the smirk in his smile I knew the genesis behind this seemingly innocent question: He was totally trying to figure out how many hours he could stay up late playing before I came back upstairs and busted him!

"Why are you asking me this?" I said, now the one smirking.

"Well, I want you to go to bed early, you know, so you can be calm and not cranky like today," he answered ever so slyly, repeating verbatim to me what I tell him often!

"Really?" I said politely, not buying a word of it.

"Well, yes and no. I think you stay up too late so um, just tell me, I'm interested." This time I indulged him—why not, right? He still had three minutes before lights out.

"I try to go to bed by 10:00, 9:30 on a good night. Now tell me, why do you really want to know?"

"Because I think you should go to bed at 7:00, like me. Because if you did, you would be a kid like me. And being a kid is fun. Way better than being a grown-up. If you were a kid you would have so much fun!"

Speechless. I was absolutely speechless.

But my mind wasn't; I couldn't stop thinking of all the things I would do if I were a kid.

If I were a kid, I would steal a Reese's Peanut Butter Cup and run and hide in the living room and eat it instead of the yucky leftovers for dinner.

If I were a kid, I would cry and cry and cry some more if my dolly and Blankie were lost or if I spilled milk on my favorite dress by accident at dinner.

If I were a kid, I would tattletale on my brother just because sometimes it was fun to get him in trouble and to feel like I was the good kid in the house.

If I were a kid, I would run around screaming, jumping, and playing tag with my friends inside because it was raining outside and I felt cooped up and totally forgot the household rules.

If I were a kid, I would ask my mommy a thousand questions to keep her from leaving me at night just so that I could have more "one-on-one" time with her. I might even ask my mommy what time she goes to bed.

And, if I were a kid, I wouldn't want to be yelled at for doing any of the above.

Nope, if I were a kid, I wouldn't want to be yelled at for just making a mistake, for still learning, for trying something new, for forgetting something simple, for just trying to have a little fun, because I know that being yelled at sucks. I know this because, even though my parents rarely yelled at me when I was a child for doing all of the above and worse, other adults in my life did; and I know I hated it and how small it made me feel. And I know it because as an adult, I have been yelled at for all those things and I know firsthand how scary, intimidating, shameful, and awful it feels. I know how much being yelled at makes me feel like a failure, like I am not good enough; I know how a yell can last only a few minutes but the shame can last for weeks; and I know that certain yells made me fear a person a lot longer than a few weeks.

Whenever our house starts to get crazy and out of control and I find myself flirting with yelling unnecessarily just to gain some resemblance of order, I push myself to remember how it feels when I get yelled at; I push myself to be empathetic and think, *"If I don't like it when I get yelled at, why would my kids like it if I yelled at them?"*

And whenever my kids start doing things one might expect from kids, I push myself to also remember that I too was once a kid and that I most certainly did everything my kids have done that has made me want to yell ... and probably worse! I stayed up late to play. I colored on the walls and actually tore a gigantic section of grass out of the grasscloth wallpaper. I made a fort out of my parents' just-made bed without asking. I too carried on at homework time and threw my pencil at my dad when he told me that X wasn't a number but was part of something called algebra. Yes, I too did things that drove my parents nuts, intentionally or not, and made them want to scream at me.

> I push myself to be empathetic and think, *"If I don't like it when I get yelled at, why would my kids like it if I yelled at them?"*

When the house is insane and all I want to do is scream, "KNOCK IT OFF ALREADY!" it is hard to remember this fact, that I once walked in my kids' shoes and did the same crap. But when I do, when I actually try and remember what I felt as a kid, I understand how my own kids might be feeling in the moment. When I try to be empathetic, it helps me understand them, it helps me stop feeling so angry and annoyed at them for something I too once did. And it helps me silence the growing yell.

If I were a kid—scratch that, when I was a kid—I was just that: a kid, just a kid learning about life and making some intentional mistakes and not so intentional mistakes along the way. But I was also a person, just like my parents. At the end of the day, kids, adults, we're all people. We all have good days and bad days. Like me, some days my kids are pleasant and sweet and listen really well; other days, they are grumpy and difficult. And like me, my kids have the same basic emotions and desire to be treated kindly. No one wants to be yelled at when he is having a bad day or even a good day. No one. Because it just doesn't feel good. Period.

Orange Rhino Revelations

- Empathy softens my desire to yell.

- Kids might truly be kids sometimes and do annoying kid stuff, but they will always be people and will always have the core desire to be treated with kindness and love.

- **I can't change that kids are people too and will have bad days, but I can love them and support them on those tough days instead of yelling at them for being human!**

Today's Actions

- **Remember, kids are people too.**

- **Focus on practicing empathy.** Put yourself in your child's shoes to understand his/her feelings. Specifically:

  - ▸ When your child acts out or is just plain annoying, ask yourself, *"Did I ever do that? Why did I do that? Did I want something? Need something? Was I just having fun? How did I want my parents to respond?"* Try to understand why your child did what he/she did so that you can relate to him/her and connect. (This will help you stay calmer and not yell.)

  - ▸ If you can't relate to the behavior (totally possible, I don't understand my boys half the time), go to the next action.

- **Recall a moment you were yelled at as a child or an adult and how it felt.** Use those awful feelings to inspire you to be warm toward your child.

- **Build your awareness of how your child feels when you yell so your empathy grows;** ask him/her to tell you how it feels or to draw a picture. Be prepared; this might make you cry. Have tissues handy. It is okay if you cry, if the answers hurt. Let the words inspire you to change, not bring you down.

> **66** **Always treat others as you** want others to treat you. **99**
>
> —The Golden Rule

Mac loves to "walk" in his daddy's shoes. His brothers have outgrown this absolutely adorable act and instead love it when I walk in their shoes and express to them that I understand what their current plight feels like.

Today's Tips

COOL	Do a random act of kindness. When I feel angry and frustrated, or just need a boost, I do something nice because the smile I receive always cools me off/warms me up!
WARM	Start a dance party; adrenaline, fun, and Mom showing off her really bad and embarrassing dance moves—what's not to love?
HOT	Bark like a dog, maybe even say, "Sit, Ubu, sit!" This will let the bark out, just not the bite. An added benefit? Your kids will probably go, "say what?!" and you'll all laugh.

Day 26

See the Good in Your Kid:
Formally Known as the Tasmanian Devil

You know the Tasmanian Devil character from the Looney Tunes cartoon? The animal that runs around and around in such a tizzy that he is always drawn with a tornado at his feet? The animal that spins through everything in sight, breaking everything in sight? The animal that eats and eats and eats and eats some more?

And did you know that they retired him as a cartoon, but that he came back to life as my son Edward? No, really, he did. You should see Edward in action when he gets all riled up and tears through the house. He runs around the house so fast and crazy, touching everything and knocking everything down on his way. And when he isn't running around screaming and creating all sorts of hoopla that drives all of us in the house absolutely mad, he is at the table. Eating. And eating. And did I mention, eating? Edward loves to eat. And to take his time eating. For as fast as he goes around the house, he goes slow when he eats. And while I know that is a good thing, a healthy thing, it drives all of us mad because normally the five of us are all done, ready to clear the dishes, and he is still chewing on his second bite, maybe his third, because he loves to take his time to savor every bite.

Yes, Edward is my Tasmanian Devil. A sweet little bugger a lot of the time, but still, a Tasmanian Devil a lot of other times. And for several years—two or three, maybe—I struggled with how to parent such a child because, honestly, when the Tasmanian Devil came out, I couldn't stand it—and that, well, that is putting it mildly. The noise, the destruction, the chaos, the upsetting any calm the others boys exhibited at the moment, the intentionally bothering all the other boys just to rile them up and try to get them to tear through the house with him, the absolutely, positively, not listening to just STOP.

"Please, Edward, STOP," I so often pleaded, trying to be the eye of the storm, the calm, rational, not destructive part of the storm. He wouldn't.

"Please, Edward, Mommy said STOP. Let's go outside," I would further plead, only to get no response except, well, a greater twinkle in the eye, a faster run, a more instigative attitude toward his brothers.

"Edward, I said STOP. STOP NOW or else …" Fill in the blank with any number of threats and consequences I tried to throw at him to stop. But he couldn't hear me; any ability to hear me, to listen to me, to respond to me, to stop had been swept up and away by his tornado. So what else could I do? What did I do?

I yelled. I yelled, and I yelled, and I yelled at him, "Just knock it off already. No one likes you when you act like this."

Yes, when Edward's Tasmanian Devil side kicked in, whether it was triggered by boredom, lack of sleep, or just a desire to play, instead of remaining as the calm center of the storm, I joined in and became destructive. Truth be told, I became more destructive than him because while his behavior was temporary, my hurtful words, my words that slowly destroyed his self-esteem, lasted longer than the moment.

How do I know? Because Edward slowly started making comments about himself like, "I can't do anything. I am a bad kid. No one likes me." Because Edward's preschool teacher noticed that he didn't have a lot of self-confidence and that he didn't believe he could do any hard tasks. Because I am his mom and I just knew it; I saw it.

But I didn't know what else to do besides getting really angry and yelling at him. He would finally be reduced to tears and that would make him stop. I felt like nothing else worked. Consequences and time-outs certainly didn't work—he just didn't *seem* to care, because he had not a care in the world, because he always saw the positive in any situation.

"Edward, you need to take a break to calm down," I would say.

"Okay, Mommy. I like sitting on the stairs because I can just look around and chill." Or, "Whatever, Mommy, I'll be up in a few minutes and then I can play again."

And when I would say, "Edward, you have lost your toy because you threw it when you went on your tear around the house," he would just say as calmly and unaffectedly as could be, "Okay, Mommy. I am lucky; I have lots of toys."

Yes, Edward always seemed unfazed by any of my attempts to rein in his behavior so that the tornado wouldn't strike again. And it maddened me. Maddened me to the point where almost all I did was criticize him and nag him, telling him to "calm down," "chill out," "behave." **Maddened me to the point where I often only complained about his behavior instead of sharing any positive reviews of his behavior. Maddened me to the point where I got so wrapped up in his weaknesses that they were all I started seeing.**

The more negative I became about the challenges of parenting a tornado, and the more negative I became about him and his behavior, the more I actively looked for the negatives in him because that was all I had on my brain. The problem with looking at the negatives is that was then all I saw. So much so, in fact, that for a brief period, I stopped seeing the numerous, abundant positives in Edward that screamed to be seen, to be recognized, to be embraced. Instead, I just thought of him as a tough kid.

I learned early on in my science education that with magnets, negative attracts positive. I wish my science teacher had then said, "But in life, negative only attracts negative, negative actually repels positive," because then maybe, maybe I would have started seeing positives earlier in life. Because then, maybe I would have stopped myself from going down the path of seeing only negative in Edward for a long period of his precious childhood. Because then, maybe I wouldn't have been so often unfair toward Edward but more loving, patient, and understanding.

Although my science teacher didn't give me the key to understanding my darling tornado, Edward's preschool teacher did. A month or so into The Orange Rhino Challenge, I sat in her office crying and said, "I just don't know what to do. I know he struggles to make friends in school because he knocks towers down. But I am struggling, too. It is taking so much energy not to yell at him and I am gonna lose it."

She passed me a tissue and said, "Look for the good and praise it. Edward has a kind, kind heart. He is passionate, loving, and thoughtful and tells the greatest stories. Catch him being good. He wants to be successful. Give him opportunities to be good. And when the tornado strikes, talk to him. Hug him. Embrace him and try to understand why he is the tornado." I went home, totally embarrassed that I cried and showed that I wasn't the "strong, put-together mom" the teacher thought I was, and decided to change. I had had enough of being a witch to my sweet son who gave me the best, tightest hugs in the world.

That night around dinner preparation time, Edward started getting antsy and I knew a tornado was brewing. I also knew he loved food, so I decided to give him an opportunity to be helpful, to be praised.

"Hey, Edward, wanna help me make the lasagna? You're a great cook, you know," I asked nervously, hopefully.

"Sure, Mom. I do LOVE lasagna," he said with a twinkle in his eye, a new kind of twinkle. It wasn't the mischievous one, but that, "Wow, I am really happy right now." **Or actually, it wasn't a new twinkle. It was the old twinkle, the one I stopped seeing, the one I stopped looking for but that always shone.**

For the rest of the week, I continued taking this approach, the looking for and telling him about his positives, the giving him chances to succeed and telling him how proud I felt. Well, the result was nothing short of AMAZING. AMAZING. Yes, all capitals—twice—to show you that I yelled that, it was just that awesome of a change! Tornadoes stopped almost completely. He listened more. He helped me, with or without being asked. He hugged more. His eyes twinkled more. And I didn't have to work so hard to not yell at him because all I wanted to do was swoop him up in hug after hug and tell him how much I loved him.

The change in him wasn't the only amazing change; I changed, too. In seeking the positives in Edward, I learned so much from him about life. I stopped seeing his carefree attitude as a pain, but instead as a reminder to relax more, to savor life more. I stopped seeing his slow eating as a nuisance, but as a reminder to slow down and enjoy the moment more. I stopped seeing his storytelling as exhausting, but instead as a reminder to be more passionate about my life experiences. And I stopped seeing his overzealous, "I just love life so much that I abound with never-ending energy" as a constant headache, but instead as a reminder to embrace life with as much gusto and positivity as he does. I am forever grateful I decided to see the positive in Edward, because not only does it overflow, but it is also truly inspirational.

I haven't called Edward the Tasmanian Devil since that week because, when I did, although it was a joke, it was actually a self-fulfilling prophecy to seek the negative. Instead, I started calling him my "Snugglebug," "My Little Chef," and "My Little Helper," because his hugs, his passion for cooking, and his desire to help me and hang out with me are some of his best traits. These traits existed when he was in his "tornado" phase of life, but I had failed to see them. I hope I don't ever lose sight of them again because they truly help me love him that much more.

Day 26: Revelations, Actions, and Tips

Orange Rhino Revelations

- Negative thinking and negative talking attract and grow negative behavior.
- **Positive thinking and positive talking attract and grow positive behavior and relationships, and lessens the desire to yell.**

Today's Actions

- **See the good in your child.** Practice the 3:1 rule. Say *at least* three things nice about your child for every correction.

  ▸ Ideally, say the three nice things *throughout* the day and not after a correction. But, if you are like me and sometimes slip with the criticism, make it right afterward. And if you don't criticize, praise yourself!

  ▸ When sharing the nice things, be specific so it shows that you aren't just being genuine, but also really noticing, paying attention, and appreciating your child. (For example, instead of "Edward, I love your picture," try "Edward, I love how you used all different colors to paint your picture.") My boys soak up really detailed comments!

- **See the good in YOURSELF while you are at it!** Remember, feeling confident about your ability to Yell Less and Love More will keep you feeling warm and fuzzy and determined. Ask yourself what three things about you are awesome and forget the criticism! Then for fun, ask your kids for three; you might just be blown away!

> **❝ Children are likely to live up**
> to what you believe of them. **❞**
>
> —Lady Bird Johnson

Today's Tips

COOL	Cook dinner that requires using your hands to squeeze. Seriously. Meatloaf, pounding chicken breasts, tearing lettuce apart. I made meatloaf one night when dinnertime was a disaster and it felt AWESOME. Just go slow and enjoy relieving the stress!
WARM	Have a good old-fashioned staring contest. Having to focus on someone's eyes is intense, but it takes the focus off yelling. And who doesn't love to stare into your child's eyes anyway and remember the first time you saw him/her?
HOT	Do robot twirls with your child, ideally outside. Put your arms out to your sides and spin the desire to yell right out of you. Collapse onto the ground with your child and refocus on what matters.

66 **If you want your children to improve,**
let them overhear the nice things
you say about them to others. 99

—Haim Ginott

Day 27

Go Back to the Basics:
Food Fight!

Cottage cheese. Just writing that word makes me cringe. Have you ever tried to clean up cottage cheese? I've tried to wipe it. I've tried to gently scoop it up. I've tried to pick it up, morsel by morsel. All it ever does is just smear and crumble and stick and make the biggest, most pain-in-the-ass mess to clean up. Oh, how I can't stand cleaning up cottage cheese and oh, how I used to yell at my boys so much for dropping it onto the floor or flinging it across the table, pretending it was snowing. Finally, I decided to stop serving it. Duh. Again, why make big problems out of little problems? I do not miss cottage cheese being in my life, not at all. Not even a morsel. I just wish that all the other food fights in my life, which show up way too frequently, could be as easily removed.

There's the standard "I-don't-like-what-you-cooked fight" that typically goes like this, and yes, all four kids always choose to complain on the same night. I mean, how else would it work, right?!

James: "My taco broke. I won't eat it!"

Edward: "I wanted a soft taco, not a hard taco, MOM!"

Andrew: "I don't like tacos anymore!"

Mac, while throwing the taco on the floor, sending meat and cheese every which way: "No, no, no!"

And there's the usual "He-has-more-than-me fight" that goes like this:

James: "Edward has more butter on his bagel than I do."

Edward: "Andrew has more orange juice than I do."

Andrew: "Mac's bagel is bigger than mine."

Mac, while sticking his finger in Edward's butter while his other hand tries to steal James's bagel: "More, more, more."

Oh, and how can I forget the one I call "the-transitive-property-of-food fight," where suddenly, just because one child doesn't like something, no one else does, even though they secretly LOVE IT.

James, pushing his plate away: "I don't like peas anymore."

Edward, taking the hint, pushing his plate away too: "I don't like peas, either."

Andrew, doing the same: "Oh yeah, me too. No peas."

And Mac, doing his version ... well, he just dumps his small bowl of peas on the floor. ARGH!

And last but certainly not the least, there is the "It's-the-end-of-the-day-and-everyone-is-wicked-tired-so-let's-yell-at-Mom-during-dinner fight." This is always my favorite:

James: "Mom, Andrew touched my leg. I can't sit next to him. Make it STOP! Make him go away! That's it, I refuse to eat dinner now."

Edward, head on the table, whining: "I'm too tired. I just can't feed myself. You feed me, Mommy."

Andrew, while crying: "Mommy, Mommy, Mommy, James hurt my feelings. And my food is touching. And I don't want dinner. I just want dessert and TV and then go to bed. Please, Mommy, PLEASE, PLEASE!"

And Mr. Mac, well when all of the above happens, he just alternates between yelling, whining, and sobbing because that is what his brothers are doing and why not copy them and add to Mommy's temporary insanity?

Yes, mealtime in our house is absolute insanity! Which really, should be of no surprise. Take food out of it for a second. All four boys are together at once, which is an instant recipe for insanity right now given their ages. And not only are all four boys together, but all four boys are in close physical proximity to each other. And all four boys want to talk to me and have all my attention at once. AHHHHHHH! Did I mention mealtime is my headache time?!

> If I know that I am going to struggle to resist the urge to yell at my kids for unacceptable mealtime behavior . . . then I put out orange napkins as a reminder to find warmth and patience.

Are there meals when we have no issues? Yes, absolutely. Are there more and more meals like that? Yes, absolutely. But are there other meals where each darling child of mine feeds off the negative energy of one other and the entire meal ends up feeling like the scene out of *Animal House* where there is one gigantic food fight and all normalcy is lost?! Um, absolutely, yes and YES! **The only difference is that food isn't thrown at my head, just cries, complaints, and yells, and all I want to do is also throw back yells and cries.** Okay, and sometimes I do want to throw back actual food because it does seem as if it would be immensely gratifying and would be a great way to relieve stress in the moment.

Anywho, when our food fights start developing, I try my hardest to rely on our family ground rules around mealtime to keep me calm and firm and not yelling. I remind my kids that unacceptable behavior will lead to eating at the counter alone. I remind my kids that food thrown is food picked up by them and dessert lost. I remind my kids that if they don't like the meal I know they like, then they can choose to not eat until the next meal.

Sometimes these reminders work like a charm. Other times, not so much. Sometimes my kiddos are just too tired to pull it together, or I am just too tired to pull it together to remind them. And for this, I am now ever so grateful for orange napkins. And not just because they help the kids clean up "not-so-accidentally" dropped and therefore "oh, can't be eaten because they fell on the floor" vegetables and other unwanted foods. Nope. Orange napkins save me from engaging in a food fight.

If I know that the meal I am serving is going to be met with a little resistance for whatever reason or if I know that I am going to struggle to resist the urge to yell at my kids

Green peas and yellow eggs flying through the air? Don't see red and get angry, see orange and feel confident that you can be warm and loving!

for unacceptable mealtime behavior or because I have my own crap going on, I had to rush to get the meal together and am flustered, I am just in desperate need of some peace and quiet and me time, then I put out orange napkins as a reminder to find warmth and patience. And on really bad days, when we are all struggling with our own issues, I put out orange plates, silverware, and cups, too. I surround us in reminders to stay calm with each other, and it works beautifully.

You know what else works beautifully for my kids and me when I know the orange reminders will need some backup? Scratching the meal altogether and just having ...

Ice cream ... or orange sherbet!

I know it's not healthy and all to serve ice cream as a meal, but I also know that sharing ice cream together when we all just need an enjoyable moment to reconnect is a lot healthier than yelling at each other and engaging in a big gigantic food fight where mean words get thrown through the air.

 **Day 27: Revelations, Actions, and Tips**

Orange Rhino Revelations

- Simple solutions do exist for some triggers (e.g., cottage cheese). This is a repeat but warrants repeating!

- Surrounding myself with orange really, truly helps me to not yell. Any and all reminders help. Another repeat, but again, it is that important to repeat!

- It is okay to sometimes "lower the bar" and not meet all my personal expectations of how I should parent (e.g., serve ice cream for dinner). The benefit of doing so is far greater than the negative impact of yelling.

Today's Actions

- **Go back to the basics talked about in chapter 1.**

- **Buy some orange napkins to use at mealtime** and/or have your child make some orange decorations for the table.

- **Review your original trigger tracking sheet to determine whether the same triggers still exist.** Do you need to track again to gain new insights and create new plans? Triggers can and will change as life does. Be honest with yourself. If new triggers exist, try to resolve them with a simple solution. If that isn't possible, try the old orange sticky notes in yelling zones to remind you to find warmth.

- **Recall my five top ways to find calm** and think of yours:
    - ▸ Let L.O.V.E. rule (listen, observe, verify, empathize).
    - ▸ Find perspective.
    - ▸ Laugh when you just want to scream.
    - ▸ Tell yourself yelling doesn't work.
    - ▸ Talk out loud and share your emotions.

> **❝ Stick with the basics, hold on to**
> your family and friends—
> they will never go out of fashion. ❞
>
> —Niki Taylor

Today's Tips

COOL	Serve orange foods and drinks for snacks throughout the day (orange juice, peaches, cheese, carrots, Cheez-Its). I wasn't joking when I said I surround myself in orange.
WARM	Pretend to have laryngitis; silence works wonders, wonders.
	Do jumping jacks to get adrenaline and endorphins going. Added bonus: Do them with your kids for a group laugh. Double added bonus: If your child is like mine and still figuring out how to get the coordination down, he will look beyond adorable and you will remember, he is just a kid, still learning.
HOT	Bang a pot or a pan; sure, it's loud at first but it gets attention, releases stress, and can lead to a fun marching band party.

Day 28

Ask Yourself Who Started It: An Ode to "Perfect" Family Portraits

I don't like turkey. Or cranberry sauce. Or any of the foods that one typically serves on Thanksgiving except for the white stuff: bread, butter, mashed potatoes, and more butter! But I love Thanksgiving Day. I love making a big, roaring fire and then cuddling up with my boys to watch the Macy's Thanksgiving Day Parade. I love "oohing and ahhing" over all the floats together and sharing stories with my boys about when I was a kid and couldn't wait to watch the parade. I love sitting down to eat and first having cranberry juice with rainbow sherbet and telling my boys that this is a tradition passed down from my great-grandmother. Oh, there is just so much to love on Thanksgiving Day.

And yet, I hated Thanksgiving 2010 because I ruined it.

I ruined it by yelling, big-time. Over a picture. A freakin' picture. Seriously?! Yes, seriously. As soon as the parade wrapped up, I deemed that it was the perfect time for the annual "Let's watch Mom jump up and down and act like a clown to make us smile" holiday card photo shoot. Yes, of course, trying to get James, Edward, and Andrew, then ages, four, three, and one, to sit still and cooperate—after they had just been sitting peacefully and quietly for an hour and just wanted to run outside and play—was the perfect time to ask them to sit still, again. And smile. And keep their hands to themselves. And try to be patient with my constant requests for, "Just one more picture, please?" I knew at the time that I was pushing my luck, given the circumstances and their ages, but yet I still pushed.

As expected, given my picture-taking history, my boys whined when I told them it was picture time. As I geared up to corral them into the living room (and to start offering bribes galore), Andrew took off as usual and ran into—of all rooms—the living room. He jumped onto the couch, laughing hysterically as he crashed into the pillows. James and Edward of course followed suit and all three boys started laughing and tickling each other and having a grand old time. So much so, that when I shouted, "Hey, look at me!" they didn't realize I had just taken a picture. It was, and still is, one of my favorite pictures in the entire world. The happiness. The love. The joy. The smiles. It melted my heart.

So you think I would have stopped right then, right? No more pictures needed, right?! Wrong. I wanted to make sure that I had the best picture. The perfect picture. I wanted to see if I could do better, even though I felt I had just been delivered a miracle. I got greedy, really, really greedy, and I asked, "One more picture, please?" They acquiesced for a few minutes, but understandably soon grew tired of my never-ending demands to sit still and smile. They had behaved wonderfully and cooperatively for so long; now they were done. They had reached their limit and started squirming, whining, pinching each other, and refusing to cooperate. So I started yelling. And I didn't stop. I didn't stop because I so badly wanted the perfect picture and I thought that yelling would force them to behave.

"Sit still!" I barked.

"Just one more! Be good!" I whined.

"WHY CAN'T YOU JUST DO THIS FOR ME?!" I yelled.

And my famous, or rather infamous, Thanksgiving 2010 line: "It's Thanksgiving, for cripe's sake! I would be so grateful for just one good picture. PLEASE! Just smile!" I yelled.

The more I yelled, the more they cried. The more they cried, the worse the pictures were, so the more I yelled. Finally, I gave up and said ever so shamefully and nastily grumbled under my breath, "That's it! I have had it. All I wanted was a picture. Thanks for nothing."

James, Edward, and Andrew then promptly ran out of the room, crying to Daddy and the grandmas. James screamed, "Mommy's a meany." Edward sobbed, "I don't like her." Andrew just cried and cried, clearly scared by how loud and nasty my voice had gotten.

> I yell at them because of me, because of my insecurities, not because of them and their inability to sit still longer than children their age should.

And I went to the bathroom and also cried and cried, feeling all the same thoughts as my kids. I pouted the rest of the day as I felt so mortified and ashamed that I had screamed at my young children for behaving as most kids would, ashamed that I had unnecessarily taken my own problem with perfection out on them. I couldn't look any of the other adults in the eye for the rest of the day. I felt so sad that my need for the perfect picture pushed me to lose it so horrifically. My guilt and shame then kept me from enjoying the holiday. **Thanksgiving is one of the days where I often feel nothing but love, and yet, that year, that year I couldn't feel it because I had yelled to the point where all I felt was hatred for myself.**

The sad thing is, that Thanksgiving wasn't the only time I felt such anger at myself for yelling at my kids over trying to get a picture. Nope, it had happened several times before. And while I sit here wanting to write that it's all just because I am a perfectionist and seek perfection in everything I do, that's a partial cop-out. It goes deeper than that.

Yes, yes, I seek the perfect picture of all my boys looking at the camera, smiling flawlessly and not picking their noses. But it's not just because I am a perfectionist; it's also because I am insecure. Oftentimes in life, I seek comfort, confidence, and reassurance that I am living a happy, good life, that I am doing good at this parenting thing, that I have happy children. And well, whenever I feel that way, I find that looking at pictures soothes my insecurities and proves to me that I am doing okay.

If I feel frustrated and down and overwhelmed by the challenges of parenting, I can look at that perfect picture and look straight into those gorgeous twinkling eyes and remember that it is all worth it, that my kids are happy and it's worth the work. If I find myself feeling sad that life is passing by too fast, my kids are growing up too fast, and I feel I have missed out, I can look at that perfect picture and remember: No, I didn't miss it, I was right there and it was wonderful. And if I feel stressed about life in general, then

> I can happily say that I now enjoy those special moments in my life even more than before because my plight for perfection and my instinct to yell aren't dampening them.

looking at pictures of my family having fun, enjoying a special vacation, enjoying a special holiday, enjoying each other helps soothe my negative mood and move me to a more positive, grateful, happy, and definitely less stressed place.

Pictures bring me comfort by helping me feel secure in this world, and rightfully or wrongfully, I rely on them for this. That is the real reason I push for perfect pictures. I don't refrain from yelling at my kids during picture time because I want the most beautiful picture ever; it's because I am afraid that if I don't get that picture, then I won't have something to look at when I need it most. I yell at them because of me, because of my insecurities, not because of them and their inability to sit still longer than children their age should.

The Orange Rhino Challenge and all the trigger digging I did helped me see this: the real reason I yelled. And by default, it helped me let go and chill out during picture time. Now when I find myself struggling to not yell at my kids when I desperately want a picture, I say to myself,

"Hey, just relax. You'll get what you get. Don't push it or you won't get a thing except crying kids, an upset you, and therefore a bad picture and a more upset you. It's not worth it! Remember, it's not them you are frustrated with; it's you. They are doing fine, you are causing the stress. Chill out. Just chill out. Remember, the goal isn't the perfect picture. It's enjoying the moment. Don't ruin it by yelling."

I can happily say that I now enjoy those special moments in my life even more than before because my plight for perfection and my instinct to yell aren't dampening them. Do I still struggle and have to push myself to let go of perfection at times? Yes. I am not perfect. But I struggle a lot less and for that I will jump up and down, act like a clown, and do all sorts of crazy things to make me smile and feel good about my progress. Because of all the things I have learned on this challenge, one most definitely is this: **It's not about perfection; it's about progress. I am making progress, and that is what matters to me more than perfection.**

Day 28: Revelations, Actions, and Tips

Orange Rhino Revelations

- Keeping my mood in a good place helps my kids stay in a good place. When I get stressed out, the kids sense it and get stressed out. When they get stressed out, I get more stressed out and eventually yell.

- It's not about perfection; it's about progress. Period. Perfection is overrated (and not just when taking pictures! It applies to parenting and learning to yell less).

Today's Actions

- **Recall my favorite line, "It's not you, it's me."** If there are yelling situations that still aren't improving, push yourself to dig deep, to go beneath what you thought the trigger was, to find the real source of stress. Create a plan for that stress. It might just be acknowledgment or acceptance, and that is okay.

- **Think of your personal goal. Is it inspiring you or stressing you out?** Is it making you feel you have to be so perfect that all you are doing is fretting and yelling? Review it and reread Day 15 if you think perhaps adjusting your goal would help you progress better. Feel no failure in doing so! Adjusting goals is part of the process.

- **Write down three achievements you have made during this journey.** Review those achievements and embrace how much progress you are making, even if you aren't feeling it.

_____

_____

_____

_____

_____

_____

- **Celebrate your progress ... seriously!** Call your support network and tell them all you have achieved. Tell your kids. Tell your friends. Scream it from the rooftops. Get celebrating—it nourishes the soul and inspires confidence and more success! (Note: I used to fear that celebrating made me arrogant, so I never did. Well, not celebrating at all was a disservice to me. It is okay to feel proud of your achievements, and it is important to share them. Go for it!)

❝ If we magnified our successes as much as we magnify our disappointments, we'd all be much happier. **❞**

—Abraham Lincoln

Today's Tips

COOL	Wear more orange! Necklaces, clothes, bracelets, hair bands, and socks. Surround yourself with orange.
WARM	Stop everything. Set the timer and declare a five-minute "me time" with no interruptions allowed.
	Snap out of it, literally. Start snapping until you no longer feel like snapping. I have to focus to be able to snap, which takes my mind off yelling.
HOT	Toot your Rhino Horn! Pretend your hand is a horn and "toot" it from your mouth. Totally blocks your mouth from yelling and reminds you that you should be tooting your horn—that you should be celebrating any and all progress so far. Feeling good about yourself is a great way to chill out.

8

Stay Determined When You Just Want to Quit

> **If you have made mistakes, even serious** mistakes, there is always another chance for you. You may have a fresh start any moment you choose, for this thing we call 'failure' is not the falling down, but the staying down.
>
> —Mary Pickford

Most of my life, when things got tough, I just quit. I didn't try to work harder. I just made excuses and walked away because that was easier, because then I wasn't set up to make mistakes or fail. And looking back, I did successfully avoid mistakes and failure a lot of the time. But I also, unfortunately, successfully created many situations that I regret because in quitting, I never gave myself the chance to succeed. And I also, unfortunately, successfully trained myself to make quitting a very natural, ingrained, and go-to behavior.

So much so that now, as an adult, when things get tough, whether it is figuring out family finances, trying to lose weight, learning to manage individual children's challenges, dealing with a marriage issue, or trying to not yell in a really challenging moment, my first inclination generally is, "Screw it, I quit! This is too hard and overwhelming. I can't do this. And I won't!" The problem is—or the blessing, if you will—is that all these adult problems I supposedly want to quit, not only can I not quit, but also I don't really want to quit; I just want them to get easier and resolved, already!

Oh, how many times did I think this while doing The Orange Rhino Challenge! In the early days, I would yell, feel like a total failure, and then feel like quitting because I had no faith that I could succeed. Or I would be exhausted after keeping cool during a child's epic tantrum, and then feel like quitting because it was such hard work. Or I would find myself stressed from my life outside of the kids and not have the patience or desire to keep it together and I would feel like quitting because I just didn't need another thing to worry about. But as you know, I didn't quit.

Because I didn't want to be a quitter anymore. Because I didn't want to quit on myself on something so important to me. Because I didn't want to quit on my kids on something so important to them. Because I didn't want to add another thing to my list of things I regret in life.

Teaching myself to find determination to keep trying during hard times took major work and determination because I was literally "unlearning" years of self-talk of "just quit, it's safer." I don't regret a minute of my efforts, though, because for as hard as it was at times to persevere and find the courage to continue, it was equally—no, MORE—rewarding to know that I overcame a huge life hurdle. Two life hurdles, actually: being a quitter and being a yeller. This chapter covers the two simple truths that helped me get back up after I fell down, and just really wanted to stay down.

Day 29

Know You Can Do It:
How to Hold a Yell

The summer after I officially completed my 365 days of The Orange Rhino Challenge, I decided that my boys and I needed a break. It had been a long couple of months and I knew that we would all benefit from some fresh air, some wireless-free connection, and some new memories in a place where I made many old and dear memories. So I loaded the boys into the minivan for a long drive to New Hampshire.

As I had learned in my seven years of parenting, and as an Orange Rhino, I knew I had my best chance of not yelling or getting grumpy if I started the trip with reasonable expectations for the drive. So, I assumed that no one would sleep and that we would need to stop every hour for someone to go pee. I mean, assuming anything else was just setting myself up to be frustrated and annoyed, right? So I mentally prepared myself for a long trek with lots of noise and lots of stops. That doesn't mean that I didn't try to make a peaceful, quick trip happen, though! Yep, I had everyone try to pee twice before we left and I timed our departure with naptime for #3 and #4.

Well, wouldn't you know it. Within fifteen minutes of driving, not one, not two, not three, but ALL FOUR of my boys were sleeping! And wouldn't you know it, an hour and a half later they were all still sleeping! Which is great, right? Miraculous even. Well yes, and no.

No, because I had drunk a cup coffee to stay awake and had forgotten to try and pee twice myself! Yes, this mama had to pee wicked bad and there was absolutely, positively no way I was going to pull over and wake up four sleeping kids to pee. Nope, wasn't gonna happen. I didn't even entertain the idea! You couldn't have paid me to pull over and end my quiet, peaceful, and easy drive up north. Sure, I had to pee so badly that I had stomach cramps, but the downside to that was far less than the upside of my boys not yelling at each other, asking me, "Are we there yet?" over and over, or complaining that they had nothing to do. Pulling over just wasn't an option. And then again, peeing in my pants wasn't really an appealing option either.

So I did what I think most parents would do in said situation; my boys slept and I squirmed.

And I squeezed my legs as close together as I could.

And I looked out the window for distractions.

And I tried to think about everything but peeing.

And I told myself over and over, *"I can do this, just a little bit longer, I can do this. If I can hold my yells, I can hold my pee!"*

And then, well then, I had an Orange Rhino moment and I laughed so hard at my absolute ridiculousness that I had to squeeze even harder because after four natural births, well, you know, sometimes pee happens.

You see, it dawned on me at that moment that learning to hold pee and learning to hold a yell are very similar.

They both take **paying attention to signals** that you are about to explode and then acting accordingly to avoid said explosion.

They both take **focus** and putting mind over matter.

They both take **practice** and doing it over and over so you can go longer and longer and **forgiveness** when accidents occur.

They both take **distractions** so that you don't think of the strong desire to do said action.

They both take **positive thinking** and telling yourself over and over that you can do it.

They both take **choosing** to do all of the above no matter how hard because the alternative is not really a desired option.

And they are both behaviors that can be learned and achieved over time!

Seriously, all ridiculousness aside and the fact that it is a wee bit crazy that I compared not yelling to not peeing in one's pants, just think about the similarities. It is kind of uncanny, right? When I stopped and realized the similarities (which, by the way, was a great distraction and kept my mind occupied on something besides the growing need to pee my brains out), I couldn't help but to think, *"Wow, all the skills that I thought I developed to not yell I didn't really just develop, I already had them and had them since I was a child when I got potty trained! I just applied them to a new situation."*

> You already have some of the skills to yell less. You already know how to work hard to control yourself physically, because you do it every day.

My point in sharing this story and risking looking like a total fool for comparing something as difficult and personal as learning to not yell to something as trivial as not peeing in one's pants is this: You already have some of the skills to yell less. You already know how to work hard to control yourself physically, because you do it every day.

Yes, the desire to yell is a heck of a lot more intense and frustrating; it's a heck of a lot more anger filled and most definitely a heck of a lot more emotionally charged. I am not in any way trying to diminish that. I guess what I am trying to say in a most absurd but also light way to combat the heaviness of yelling as a topic is that … you can do it.

You can yell less.

You have the skills within you already! When you feel like you are struggling, just remember what you already know:

1. Pay attention to your personal signals that a yell (just like a pee) is coming on so that when you feel them the next time you know to run to the bathroom and scream in the toilet instead of exploding at the kids.

2. Focus all your energy on one task, one goal—yelling less. Focusing on too many goals at once is too much stress.

3. Practice not yelling over and over again and forgiving yourself if you slip up. Accidents happen, trust me—since my fourth son was born I have had two pee accidents. But hey, it happened and I learned that I need to focus harder on not laughing on a full bladder! So if an accident does happen and you do yell, forgive yourself. Let the shame and embarrassment go and know that there will be another opportunity to practice and succeed.

4. Set yourself up for success by placing distractions around the house, or rather, reminders to not yell. Place pictures of the kids in yell zones (great way to feel love, not anger) if you haven't already, and put up Orange Rhinos to remember to be warm and calm.

5. Be positive and believe in yourself. Tell yourself over and over, "I am calm and I won't yell."

6. Choose to not yell because you know yelling does not work and just isn't a good option. Choose to hold it together, to squirm, and to squeeze your hands in frustration instead of yelling. Choose to try your hardest even on days when you want to scream your brains out.

7. Tell yourself that you are learning to yell less and that it takes time, just like potty training, but that it can happen and will happen! I wasn't born knowing how to hold my pee or, um, other things. Just ask my parents or the nice couple at the beach sharing a romantic picnic. I may or may not have walked over to them totally naked at age two and squatted on their blanket and left them a present. Like, a smelly one. Moving right along … Seriously, it takes time to learn how to not yell, but it can be done.

Okay, it's official. This story is weird. I just told you that I pooped on a blanket as a kid and that I have pee accidents at the age of thirty-something. If nothing else is achieved from this story, I hope you are laughing with me and have a newfound sense of determination to push forward because you believe that you can do it!

Orange Rhino Revelations

- Saying, "Yes, I did it!" always feels amazing! Whether it is making it an extra thirty minutes without peeing or making it thirty minutes without yelling, I have never said, "Ugh, I did it!" I have never regretted working hard and trying. Never.

- Teaching myself to not yell is not a new experience, per se—I have had to teach myself a lot of skills in life and I have successfully done so (learning to drive, passing tests in school, learning to hold my tongue and respect my bosses, and so on). I have done hard things before and I can do this.

- My love for my kids is one of the greatest motivating factors ever.

- I can do hard things.

Today's Actions

- **Remind yourself that YOU CAN DO IT, that you can Yell Less and Love More.** If needed, brainstorm all the hard things in your life that you have done, remembering that there is no success too small.

- **Embrace this other embarrassing bathroom analogy.** When I am at a party/concert/ ballgame/event and I break to go to the bathroom, I then have to go all night. But if I hold it, then I can enjoy the party longer with fewer breaks. Am I right? The same goes for yelling. When I have snapped, the snaps just come easier and easier and easier because the floodgates are open and because I think, "Eeck, I made a mistake, there goes the entire day."

- **Stop the floodgates of snapping and yelling by saying,** "Okay. I snapped/yelled. That moment has passed. The day is not ruined. New moment starts NOW."

- **Keep the floodgates closed by immediately forgiving yourself and by engaging in a positive activity** to get you back on track: Take care of you for a few minutes or play with kids.

66 Whether you think you can,
or you think you can't—you're right. **99**

—Henry Ford

Today's Tips

COOL	Go for a walk outside; fresh air always brings fresher, cleaner moods.
WARM	Smile! Rumor has it that if you fake it, you'll feel it! So fake feeling happy and find the anger recede.
	Eat frozen grapes and pretend for a second kids are sleeping and the grapes are wine. Okay, it's a stretch. But I did do this once and reaching into the freezer snapped me out of my mood!
HOT	Count to 10; or 100; or 1,000 until you calm down. (Note: I can't stand counting, but I have done it, and it works!)

Day 30

Remember What Matters: Tipping the Scale Toward Love

520.

That is the number of days I consecutively went without yelling. The streak ended on July 12, 2013, when I totally lost it and yelled at my boys BIG-time. There was no question if it was maybe just a snap or an emergency yell. Oh no, it was a full-on, blood-curling, yelling tirade complete with four children bawling and one mommy who just couldn't stop herself. And it was topped off with my feeling guilty, disappointed, and sad beyond belief. Hearing my boys scream back at me just made me feel worse.

"Mommy! You're so mean. You're back to day zero on your challenge!" screamed James.

"Too loud!" cried Andrew, as he covered his ears.

"Ma Ma. Ma Ma," sobbed Mac, who up until that moment had never, ever heard me yell.

"Why are you ye ... ll ... ing at us, Mommy? We ddd ... idn't do an ... y ... thing! We got in the car like you asked!" Edward tried to say between sobs.

Edward was right. Oh, was he right. My boys had done absolutely, positively, nothing wrong. I was just in a mood. My yell was completely unnecessary, completely hurtful, and completely my own doing. I took my own sadness, fear, and anger out on them, period. The stress of my marriage and life and parenting combined with my complete and utter lack of sleep and exercise finally got to me. As a result, everything bothered me that morning.

The boys talking in normal voices? Too loud.

The boys asking me for some water? Too demanding.

The boys roughhousing and laughing? Too much, what, too much being kids?

The boys not getting ready for the pool when I asked? Too much, what, not listening when I mumbled my request under my breath so quietly no one could hear it?

I felt my anger bubbling up and my sweaty hands, my racing heart, and my shorter and sharper voice told me that I was flirting with losing it, that I was in desperate need of getting in control. So I tried. I tried so very hard to get in control of my personal stress by pulling out some of my Orange Rhino tricks. I talked to myself, *"Hey, Orange Rhino, you are not mad at the kids, you are frustrated with your situation right now."* I got a glass of cold water and physically tried to cool down and slow my breathing. I talked to myself some more: *"You can do this, you will get through this; just hang on, you don't want to yell."* And I talked to my kids. "Boys, Mommy is having a tough morning. I am feeling a little grouchy. Can you stop running around and help me get ready for the pool fast so we can go have fun and relax?"

It worked.

For like five minutes.

For five minutes I found calm amidst the crazy, I found warmth amidst my anger, I found determination amidst my desire to just quit and scream. The boys stood in line for lotion, grabbed their towels, put their shoes on, and got in the car. Yes! I went in the house to get my bag and came back to find kids not buckled in as requested.

And I lost it. In my loudest voice ever (or maybe it felt so loud because it had been 520 days since I'd heard it?) I screamed, "WHAT ON EARTH DO YOU THINK YOU ARE DOING?! WHY ARE YOU NOT BUCKLED IN? WHAT IS WRONG WITH YOU? CAN'T YOU JUST LISTEN FOR ONCE?!"

Seriously? I mean, really just writing that, I feel ridiculous and ashamed. After everything they had JUST done to be helpful and wonderful I lost it because they didn't do one of five things I had asked them? Was that necessary? Or even nice? No! But then again, I didn't yell because they didn't put their seatbelts on.

I yelled because my own pain and frustration screamed to get out.

I yelled because, well, because I am human and sometimes, despite best intentions, hard work, and a heart full of more love than ever, mistakes happen. Yells happen. And when yells do happen, unfortunately they can't be taken back. They can't be erased. They can, however, make a day go even more downhill or turn around completely.

> I yelled because, well, because I am human and sometimes, despite best intentions, hard work, and a heart full of more love than ever, mistakes happen. Yells happen.

When I finally stopped yelling, I found myself frozen, worried yet curious as to how I would respond. Would I crumple to the floor in absolute self loathing, disgust, and disappointment? Would I quickly find myself in the vicious cycle of negative self-talk that would by default keep me yelling over and over and over, making the day go downhill rapidly? Would I let the one yell destroy the entire day and all the opportunities to enjoy my children, which I totally would have done—no, wait, did do—520 days prior?

Or would I embrace all that I had learned on my 520-day journey and do what I had told so many other Orange Rhinos but had yet needed to tell myself? **Would I accept that it was okay that I wasn't perfect, that parenting isn't about perfection, but about doing the best we can in any given moment? Would I choose to forgive myself, as I often advised, and move forward, driven by the undisputable truth that every moment is a new moment, a new opportunity to create a loving memory with my children, despite what happened the moment prior?**

I stood in front of my minivan, tears still dripping down my face, sweat still forming in my hands, pain still pounding in my rapidly beating heart, and wondered, would I choose to focus on the negative immediate moment or the bigger picture, that at the end of the day, what matters most isn't perfection but that the number of loving moments outweighs the not-so-loving moments?

I chose forgiveness.

I chose moving forward.

I chose to remember the big picture.

I chose to focus on creating more loving moments the rest of the day so that I could tip the relationship scale toward love, not anger.

Believe it or not, once I decided to move forward, I felt quite grateful and relieved. Not grateful because I had yelled, of course, but grateful that I had changed so much that I now had the perspective and courage to start fresh the next moment, to let go of the past so that it didn't dampen the future. This was a huge change for me—like, gigantic. Like so totally supercalifragilisticexpialidocious that I actually found myself smiling in that moment, not crying. The Orange Rhino Challenge had changed me. So many of those negative personal qualities that used to bring me down had lessened, if not completely disappeared. My life was full of so much more love for my kids, my family, and myself. Again, I couldn't stop smiling.

> I chose to focus on creating more loving moments the rest of the day so that I could tip the relationship scale toward love, not anger.

I hugged my kiddos and apologized and we went off for the day, bound and determined to have a fun time, bound and determined to have a day filled with more love and less anger. Every once in a while my mind would slip from the moment and think of the morning when I lost it. Disappointment and fear that my yell had erased all the good moments from the past 520 days tried to get a front and center seat in my mind. But I fought back.

I reminded myself that love trumps anger.

I reminded myself that one moment of anger is nothing compared to 520 days of loving more. I reminded myself that every moment from that morning forward that I choose love is a win. I reminded myself that all the loving moments from here on out would add up and add up and add up to the point that all the new positive memories would push away the angry, negative one from July 12, 2013.

And I reminded myself why I chose to let go of the past and enjoy the moment now: my fierce, passionate, overwhelming love for four beautiful boys named James, Edward, Andrew, and Mac.

I want my boys to look back at their childhood, their life, and say, "Yes, my parents loved me and I felt their love more often than their wrath. I feel really blessed." This is my ultimate goal as a parent, as an Orange Rhino. To love more. And this is ultimately what kept me determined to not succumb to "failure" that July morning. I am an Orange Rhino and I will Yell Less and Love More, one moment at a time.

Orange Rhino Revelations

- Parenting isn't about perfection; it's about loving my kids the best I can in any moment.

- Teaching my children is part of loving them. Showing them that I am not perfect, that mistakes happen, and that getting up and finding the courage to learn from them and continue, despite discouragement, are invaluable lessons.

- Being an Orange Rhino isn't about perfection; it's about yelling less and loving more, one moment at a time, so that there are more loving moments in a child's life than angry moments, so that the scale is tipped heavily toward love.

Today's Actions

- **Tip the scale toward love today.** Make at least one really loving moment with your children happen, no matter what. Especially if it feels like a crazy, rushed, stressed day. Loving moments are the greatest way to not fall in the yelling trap. (I wish I had stopped and connected with my kiddos that July morning. I missed that piece!)

- **Ask your children, "How can I show you my love today?"** Sometimes loving our kids is doing what we know we should do; other times, it's doing what they want us to do (or at least a version of it, as I am sure letting my son eat candy all day would be his answer).

❝ To live is to choose. But to choose well, you must know who you are and what you stand for, where you want to go, and why you want to get there. ❞

—Kofi Annan

Today's Tips

COOL	Wear an orange bracelet around your wrist to remember your promise, or as Andrew says, tie an orange ribbon around your finger!
WARM	Put earbuds in your ears and listen to music; sometimes I put on music from my baby shower to remind me how excited (and not angry!) I felt before each birth.
HOT	Ask your kids what you look like in the moment; their words might hurt but will more likely help you pull it together.

9

Beyond Day 30

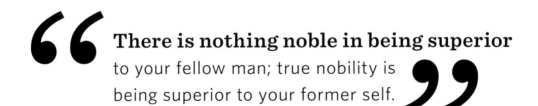

There is nothing noble in being superior to your fellow man; true nobility is being superior to your former self.

—Ernest Hemingway

On February 6, 2013, the day I officially completed Day 365 of not yelling, I remember thinking to myself, *"Okay, so now what?"* Well, seeing as I went 520 days, you know what I decided. I kept going, trying to extend my promise to be an Orange Rhino as long as possible beyond my goal.

And I remember on July 13, 2013, when I officially made it through another day without yelling, thinking to myself, *"Okay, so I started again. Does this mean I am committing to another year, or given my 520-day streak, that I am aiming beyond 520 days? Um, that is really intense. And scary."* This last story and the quotation by Ernest Hemingway should give you a clue to my answer. And hopefully, both will inspire you to keep your personal journey to Yell Less and Love More extend beyond these last few pages.

Every Day Past 30: My Promise to My Boys

Edward often likes to sit on the chair near my closet and have little chitchats with me in the morning while I get ready. He varies his starting questions but somehow he always ends up at the same three:

"Mommy, why do you still have a baby in your belly?"

"I don't, sweetie, that's just the way my belly looks now," I reply.

"Oh. Okay. Then when will you have another baby in your belly? Don't you want a girl too?"

"I love you boys. Sure, it might be nice to have a sister for you guys, but I think four is good and I wouldn't trade any one of you for the world," I reply.

"Oh. Okay. Well, why did you only make boy babies?"

That's my favorite because I always laugh and reply with, "Because when I met your daddy, he wanted boys so badly that every time we passed a fountain he threw in all the quarters he had and wished for you!"

"Oh. Okay. Bye."

And just like that he scampers out, totally done with the conversation.

One day, though, shortly after I celebrated 365 days of not yelling, he changed it up a bit. As I put my engagement and wedding rings on, Edward said to me, "Mommy, why do you wear those rings?"

"Well," I said, "the sparkly one is called an engagement ring. Daddy gave it to me one night when he asked me to marry him and spend my life with him. He gave it to me as a promise to marry me and love me forever. I wear it as a promise to marry him and love him forever."

"Oh, okay. It's pretty. And the other ring?" he asked, totally engrossed.

"That's my wedding ring. Daddy put it on my finger the day we actually got married. He has one too that I gave him. We wear our rings to show our commitment to each other, to be nice to each other, to love each other on good days and on not-so-good days," I said.

Edward's eyes widened; I could tell he was about to blow me away with one of his totally sweet, totally shocking statements. And he did.

"Mommy, where's my engagement ring?" he said.

"Excuse me?" I asked.

"Where's my ring? Why don't you wear a ring for us kids showing your promise to love us forever?

Wow. Wow. Wow. Edward's question was so innocent, so amazing, and so thought provoking. I didn't know how to answer; there was no good answer. So I simply said, "Edward, that is a really good question. You make a really good point. I should have a ring to show my promise to love you and your brothers forever, shouldn't I?"

"Yep. Yep, you should, Mommy," he said.

And just like that he scampered off, totally done with the conversation.

I, however, wasn't. I couldn't move on, figuratively and literally. I stood outside my closet, so awestruck from the poignancy of the conversation that I couldn't get myself to turn around and get dressed for the day. Fighting from the hallway solved that problem right away, though! Motivated to get a move on before things got ugly, I turned around to my closet to get dressed. I went to pick a shirt and saw nothing but orange. Orange T-shirts. Orange long-sleeve shirts. Orange sweaters. I started smiling and immediately thought, *"I might not have a ring to show my commitment and love to my boys, but I have a closet full of orange clothes to show it!"*

And I still do, months and months after I successfully met and surpassed my original Orange Rhino Challenge goal, and months and months after orange was no longer the "hot" color. Orange might go off trend in the fashion world, but in my house it never will.

Orange will always be a favorite color because I will always be an Orange Rhino.

I promised my boys since the day each of them was born that I would always love them. Now, more than ever, I know that loving them forever means being committed to being an Orange Rhino, forever.

It means continuing to focus daily on my promise despite my original success so that I don't get overconfident of my "skills" and slip into old habits.

It means continuing to remind myself of all that I learned on my journey so that I can keep practicing and practicing not yelling, so that it becomes even more and more natural.

It means continuing to wear orange shirts and post positive phrases on orange sticky notes so that I keep my promise front and center where it belongs, where I want it to be. And where I will need it to be as life changes, as I change, as my kids change and I need reinforcement and inspiration to keep my yelling away.

It means continuing to track and review triggers when said changes do occur and I find myself struggling in new ways and I need a new path and a new plan to keep me true to my promise.

And, it means continuing to soul search and ask myself the hard questions so that, as I grow as a parent and as a person, I can still understand and nurture myself as necessary to keep me in a loving place.

Being an Orange Rhino forever doesn't mean that I will focus on perfection. No, it just means that I will never stop trying to do my best every day, both on good days and on not-so-good days. It means I will never stop trying to improve who I am and my skills as an Orange Rhino. It means I will never stop trying to show my warmth, not my wrath; to choose kind words, not harsh words; to Yell Less and Love More, one moment at a time, because not only is that what my kids deserve, but it is also what I want to give them with all my heart and soul.

❝ Dare to live the life you have
dreamed for yourself. Go forward
and make your dreams come true. ❞

—Ralph Waldo Emerson

10

Summary
of Key Points

Each day that passed on my Orange Rhino Challenge, not yelling became easier and more natural because of a core set of revelations about yelling, alternatives to keep from yelling, and benefits of not yelling, that I could readily rely on for success. I share these with you so that on days when not yelling feels anything but easy, you at least have an quick and easy way to find inspiration and guidance.

Top 10 Orange Rhino Revelations About Yelling

1. Yelling doesn't work; in fact, it often makes matters worse. L.O.V.E.ing my kids—listening, observing, verifying, and empathizing—works much better. It allows me to actually help my kids calm down, focus, and listen from a good place, not a resentful, you-scared-me, I-don't-like-you place. It is then, not when I am yelling, that my kids can actually hear what I have to say, what I want to teach them.

2. I can't always control my kids' actions, but I can always control my reaction. I have a choice to yell or not to yell; I have a choice to walk away and take a break or to break all hearts involved by yelling.

3. Often, I am the source of the problem, not my kids. Self-awareness is a sobering, but enlightening, experience. Without it, I probably wouldn't have succeeded. I daily dare myself to look inside and ask, *"Why am I really yelling?"* when I find myself in a rut. The answer often gets me out.

4. Taking care of me, prioritizing "me time," isn't selfish; it's crucial. If I want to be in a good, loving place where I can easily control my yells, I need to take care of me. Period. And if I need help achieving some me time, I need to ask for it and not be ashamed.

5. Positive thoughts, actions, and statements attract positive behavior. Negative actions just attract and grow more negative actions. This applies to both interactions with my children and with myself!

6. Parenting isn't about perfection, but about progress. Mistakes happen. It's what I do afterward that's more important than the mistake. I forgive myself, I apologize to my kids, and I try to learn from what happened so I can progress forward. Otherwise, I just get in a yelling rut.

7. Knowing my physical symptoms of a growing yell is huge! Sweaty palms, racing heart, twitching body, rising voice—all these things let me know I am getting ready to lose it; I need to pay attention to them!

8. Perspective is a powerful tool. When I find all the small stuff is getting to me, and even some of the big stuff, I look for perspective to ground me and use the words "at least" to help out. It's just spilled milk; at least it wasn't the entire jug!

9. Kids are people too. Like me, kids have feelings. Like me, kids don't want to be yelled at. Like me, my kids are still learning. Putting myself in my kids' shoes helps me treat them as I would want to be treated.

10. Good things happen when I don't yell. Whether it's extra hugs, extra spontaneous "I love yous," or extra special conversations, good things happen if I keep it together.

Top 10 Benefits of Being an Orange Rhino

1. I feel calmer and more peaceful in my heart and in my home. Yelling revs everyone up. Without it, I walk more gently, I speak more gently, and I am not polluting the house and myself with anger. Calmness is contagious!

2. My kids respond better to me (most of the time). I am not going to write that I stopped yelling and the kids became perfect. Nope, they are human like me! But, they do generally respond faster, more accurately, and more sweetly now and tantrums are shorter and less intense.

3. I have more fun with my children. Without all the negative energy, I am in a better place to enjoy the moment and to make enjoyable moments happen. And, if I happen to be in a bad mood, I now look to share a fun moment with my kiddos because I discovered that connecting with them is one of the greatest bad-mood shakers.

4. I let go, I stop ruminating, much faster and much more easily. This is one of the greatest gifts of the challenge. I used to let problems eat away at me, my confidence, my happiness, and my ability to enjoy my children. Learning to manage this trigger is a benefit I will forever be grateful for.

5. I take care of me without feeling guilty. Now, I never feel regret when I take care of me, just pride that I found the awareness and strength to do so.

6. I am teaching my kids to manage anger. I love that my boys now do some of my alternatives to yelling instead of lashing out verbally or physically when they are in a mood.

7. I am much, much better at handling being overwhelmed. I made it through tough "I just want to yell" days by going one moment at a time, and I now apply this approach more readily when I am feeling overwhelmed by any task. This new approach sure makes life more manageable and therefore also helps with not yelling.

8. I do more random acts of kindness. When I stopped yelling, I felt kinder and naturally wanted to share the kindness. I started doing random acts of kindness as frequently as earlier in my life and it feels fantastic! I also started doing them on tough days because I knew they would make me feel better: a total win-win!

9. I naturally apply all I have learned to all my relationships. I have wanted to yell at many an adult since I started The Orange Rhino Challenge. But I didn't, not just because I knew it wouldn't achieve anything but an angrier me, but also because it was more natural not to yell. Having more calm interactions in my life in general is a godsend!

10. I have more faith in myself that I can do hard things. I used to be a quitter when the going got tough. I now no longer see myself as a quitter, but as someone who can persevere. When a tough situation arises, I find myself saying, *"You taught yourself not to yell. You can do this!"*

Top 10 Alternatives to Yelling

1. Talking to myself and saying, *"I can do this, I can do this,"* or *"Orange Rhino, Orange Rhino, Orange Rhino!"*

2. Putting my hands in the air to get attention while taking a deep breath. Or a hundred.

3. Letting the ugly words that are on the tip of my tongue come out as gibberish: "Oogaschmoogaboga!"

4. Closing my eyes and picturing myself on a beach, drink in hand, listening to the ocean.

5. Staring at baby pictures of my boys and remembering that they are fragile and I need to proceed gently.

6. Running to the bathroom, shutting the door, and yelling into the toilet.

7. Saying out loud, "It's gonna be a great day!" while smiling just like the announcer in the movie *Jerry Maguire*. I laugh and find myself believing my words.

8. Grabbing a washcloth, running it under warm water, and then washing my frustration away from my face.

9. Eating something crunchy such as an apple or carrots. This is tied with squeezing something hard (Play-Doh, towel, hands, counter).

10. Stopping what I am doing and hugging, laughing, or playing with my kids.

Add your favorite alternatives to yelling here. Note which ones work best in certain situations.

_____

_____

_____

_____

_____

_____

_____

_____

_____

_____

Most Frequent Orange Rhino Triggers and Solutions

Trigger	Solutions To Turn To
Bedtime Frenzy	• Remind myself that rushing and yelling makes bedtime take longer. • Wet a washcloth and wash my face (as they do in spas to relax). • Light an aromatherapy candle or use aromatherapy lotion. • Dim the lights and pretend I am at a spa. • Remind myself that I want to end the day on a loving note.
Feeling Overwhelmed	• Tell myself to go one moment at a time; take deep breaths when not talking to myself. • Tell myself that I can do this. • Take a short break for some me time. • Exercise; push-ups and jumping jacks are quick, easy, and effective.
Feeling Tired	• First and foremost, put kids and myself in orange clothes as walking reminders to be an Orange Rhino. • Get fresh air. • Schedule a preventive yell with the kids; run outside at a park yelling and screaming so it gets out before it slips out. • Cross my fingers and hope I make it through the day (what can I say, this is a brutal trigger!).

Trigger	Solutions To Turn To
Individual Child Trait	• Look for the positive in the child and embrace it; talk about it to yourself, share it with your child. • Create an opportunity for child to succeed (e.g., helping me). • Remind myself that we are all human and not perfect; remind myself that I too can be difficult. • Spend quality time with that child or if really challenging at the moment, take a break from each other.
Mealtime	• Surround myself with orange. Period. Orange napkins, orange plates, orange silverware. Orange foods. If I sense a mealtime is going to be a disaster, I bring in the reinforcements. • Turn the lights out and light a candle and tell children they are in a fancy restaurant, the kind Mom and Dad "go" to (okay, dream of going to). Play quiet music if needed.
Messy Bedroom (also applies to any standard-ish expected child behavior that he/she is learning to manage)	• Put all small toys in under the bed sweater bins. No more dumping and sorting on the floor, where my feet are attacked. My sons now pull out their bins, sort in them, build in them, then push them back under the bed. Out of sight, out of mind. • Find perspective. It is just a messy room. It is not worth yelling over. Getting frustrated and annoyed? Okay. Yelling? No. Besides, staying calm and stating what needs to happen and why has a much better chance of getting the room clean then and in the future. • Help my child if needed; in other words, remind myself that we all need help sometimes and that teaching my son to ask for help is just as important as teaching him to do things on his own. • Review my expectations; given my child's age, am I asking too much at that moment?

Trigger	Solutions To Turn To
Morning Rush	• Prepare as much as I can the night before. • Put orange sticky notes at the back door and near backpacks as a reminder to "Stop!" and find warmth. • Remind myself that yelling won't get us to school faster, but will increase chances of being late. • Remind myself that being late isn't the end of the world, but actually a good lesson, for everyone.
Not Listening	• Remind myself that yelling won't make my kids listen or respond any better, that it will just make them tune me out. • Ask myself, *"Was my request specific, simple, and doable?"* If not, redo! • Ask myself, *"Did I deliver my request as best as I could?"* (Did I get attention first, was I close enough to be heard?) If not, redo! • Have my child repeat back request so I know he heard it and understood it. • Remind myself of Robert Fulghum's quotation, "Don't worry that children never listen to you; worry that they are always watching you." This helps me respond calmly and effectively.
Personal Problems	• Tell myself, *"I am not mad at the kids, I am frustrated by ... (fill in problem)."* Then direct my energy toward resolving the real problem or deciding to let go of it. • Express my emotions (in a child-appropriate manner) and ask for some space. If I can't get space, get outside to a park. • Call a friend and let the frustration out if it is still triggering me; then tell myself when I hang up the phone the problem is on hold until after bedtime.

Frequently Asked Questions and Answers

1. What about in case of emergencies, do you yell then?

Yes, I do. If a child is in danger (running into street, touching hot stove, about to fall), then I do raise my voice to the yell level so I can get attention fast. But, I make sure that I yell *to* my child, not *at* him. To me, there is a distinct difference. Yelling *at* someone generally means that hurtful and shameful words fly out. But when you yell *to* someone, the intent is to get attention, not to be harmful. When I do use an "emergency yell," I keep it simple: "Stop! Danger!" The benefit of not yelling is that when I do need to actually yell for safety, I am taken very seriously, it is very effective, and I have my kids' full attention to deliver a key safety lesson.

2. How do you discipline without yelling?

I believe that disciplining my children means teaching them. I learned rather quickly that I can't teach my children when I am yelling at them for two reasons: 1) I am yelling and am unintelligible, so my kids don't stand a chance of understanding what I am trying to say and therefore they can't learn, and (2) if I am yelling, my kids shut down and tune me out and become unable to learn from me (as I do when people yell at me). If I want to truly discipline my children, I am best served by not yelling but waiting until we are both calm so that I can deliver my message clearly and they can hear me and take in what I have to say without a problem.

I know the next question is, okay then, so how do you teach your children right from wrong? To be honest, I am a work in progress. I am trying to find the balance between natural consequences and positive reinforcement. I find that the more positive I am toward my children (not to be read as overly praising them, but as not overly criticizing them) the better they receive and embrace what I have to say. I also try to teach them by modeling the behavior I want them to embrace.

3. Help! My partner and other family members and caretakers aren't on board with my goals and keep yelling at the kids. What do I do?

This is a very popular question and I always say, "Stick to your beliefs and model how not yelling can work. Once the results become more and more apparent (and remember, be patient as you wait for the results), your partner/family members will see the benefits and will be inspired. And if not, remember that what matters is more loving moments in your child's life. You are making that happen. Loving moments from you and yelling moments from your partner/family members is still better than yelling moments from all partners. Hang in and have faith that they will come around!"

Another solution? Have your kids say "Orange Rhino" to the partner/family member to help bring attention to his/her behavior. My children once Orange Rhino'ed Grandpa and he was flabbergasted! He promised them that he would do better, and he did!

4. The alternatives all seemed geared to younger kids—they so wouldn't work in my house. Suggestions?

The goal of my alternatives are:

- to make learning to yell less more fun,
- to find ways to calm myself down,
- to surprise my children so I can get their attention, and
- to diffuse a frustrating moment and refocus us all.

If you find that they aren't working for you or that you feel uncomfortable doing them, brainstorm some other ideas that fit into the above buckets. Be creative, be silly, and think outside of the box! I also suggest trying them anyway; you might be surprised to find that they do work.

5. Help! I have tracked my triggers and I am trying my hardest, but I am still struggling! What do I do?

- Don't give up!
- Remind yourself that you are unlearning a tough habit and it takes time.
- Tell yourself that you have already made progress just by trying to change and that you are well on your way.
- Celebrate any small step you think is a baby step (e.g., tracking triggers, yelling one less time a day than usual) because baby steps are big steps and deserve celebration.
- Dig deeper. Ask yourself, are you being as honest as you can be about your triggers?
- Find support, and if your current support network isn't as encouraging as need be, find new support.
- Make sure you are taking care of you, loving you, and forgiving you after tough days.
- Review your goal. Make sure that it is inspiring but not so far out of reach that it is debilitating. Consider adjusting it so that you get a win under your belt and more confidence.
- Believe that you can do this. Because you can. If yelling less and loving more truly matters to you, which I am sure it does, you will make it happen. Just give yourself the time, patience, and self-love to let it happen.

Resources

To help you on your journey to Yell Less and Love More I have included here a blank version of my favorite tool, the **Orange Rhino Tracking Sheet,** along with instructions on how to use it. Make multiple copies to keep you on track throughout your journey.

On the back flap of this book you will find the **Orange Rhino Sign,** to be used by kids to remind you, "Stop! Don't yell!"

• The Orange Rhino Trigger Tracking Sheet

You can find even more support and resources at:

• My blog, www.TheOrangeRhino.com

• Our online forum, www.TheOrangeRhino.com/community (case sensitive)

• Our Facebook community, www.facebook.com/TheOrangeRhino

The Orange Rhino Trigger Tracking Sheet

How to use this tool:

1. Write down anytime you yell or want to yell and fill in as many columns as possible and be detailed. Also note when you wanted to yell but didn't so you can see your progress! Note these entries with an asterisk (*).

2. At the end of the day review the chart and **circle** any trends (e.g. repeated emotions, repeated times of day). This will help you quickly spot "trouble" areas that need focus.

3. After several days of tracking, **underline** any triggers that are fixable, **highlight** triggers that are manageable, and **box** triggers that are unchangeable. Remember the following to help you group your triggers.

- **Fixable Triggers:** Think of these as the easy ones, the quick wins where an easy solution exists to remove the trigger completely. Examples: morning rush (pack bags night before), noise (wear earmuffs), kids forgetting morning routine (post picture schedule in bedroom).

- **Manageable Triggers:** These triggers aren't always present but you can learn to prepare for them so that when they do pop up, you can manage your response. In some cases, with enough practice, they might even become close to extinct as a trigger. Examples: fight with spouse, PMS, children fighting, being tired.

- **Unchangeable Triggers:** These are the triggers that are out of your control because you can't remove them from your life, either at all or under the timetable you wish. They probably challenge you daily. Examples: health issues, past traumatic events, other people's behavior. They don't need to be huge: They might be as simple as "husband won't make bed."

Follow along with the book for how to proceed from here. If you have finished the book and are coming back to track triggers again because you have found that with life changing, triggers changed, I suggest that you follow steps 1 through 3 again. After you group your triggers, pick one at a time and go after it. When you have mastered that trigger, pick another. Happy Tracking!

THE ORANGE RHINO CHALLENGE TRIGGER TRACKING EXAMPLE SHEET

Day and time	Whom I yelled at	Supposed Trigger	How I felt at the time? Anything bothering me?	What was I doing before I felt the urge to yell?	What were kids doing, if applicable?	Were kids hungry, thirsty, tired?	Did I feel any physical symptoms before?	What could I have done better?
6:45 a.m.	Andrew	Whining, but really I was just tired	N/A	Getting Mac dressed	N/A	Thirsty	N/A	Set out drink cups night before
***8:13 a.m.	James	Screwing around	Rushed to get to school on time	Running around making breakfast	N/A	N/A	Sweaty	Pack snacks night before
8:53 a.m.	All of them!	Kids won't put shoes on for school	Rushed, frustrated, tired	Looking at BlackBerry, multitasking. I guess the real trigger is I wasn't present.	Playing happily	No, but they were preoccupied	N/A	Put BlackBerry down, help them, give 5 minutes warning
6:05 p.m.	James, Edward, Mac	Won't go upstairs	Rushed, tired. Mad that there aren't enough hours in the day.	Cleaning up	Watching TV happily	Tired	Racing heart	Give warning, put cleaning off until later so I'm not rushing

Takeaways: Morning rush an issue. I clearly need more sleep. When I am preoccupied and don't give directions eye to eye I might as well be talking to a wall!

THE ORANGE RHINO CHALLENGE TRIGGER TRACKING SHEET

Day and time	Whom I yelled at	Supposed Trigger	How I felt at the time? Anything bothering me?	What was I doing before I felt the urge to yell?	What were kids doing, if applicable?	Were kids hungry, thirsty, tired?	Did I feel any physical symptoms before?	What could I have done better?

Takeaways:

THE ORANGE RHINO CHALLENGE TRIGGER TRACKING SHEET

Day and time	Whom I yelled at	Supposed Trigger	How I felt at the time? Anything bothering me?	What was I doing before I felt the urge to yell?	What were kids doing, if applicable?	Were kids hungry, thirsty, tired?	Did I feel any physical symptoms before?	What could I have done better?

Takeaways:

THE ORANGE RHINO CHALLENGE TRIGGER TRACKING SHEET

Day and time	Whom I yelled at	Supposed Trigger	How I felt at the time? Anything bothering me?	What was I doing before I felt the urge to yell?	What were kids doing, if applicable?	Were kids hungry, thirsty, tired?	Did I feel any physical symptoms before?	What could I have done better?

Takeaways:

THE ORANGE RHINO CHALLENGE TRIGGER TRACKING SHEET

Day and time	Whom I yelled at	Supposed Trigger	How I felt at the time? Anything bothering me?	What was I doing before I felt the urge to yell?	What were kids doing, if applicable?	Were kids hungry, thirsty, tired?	Did I feel any physical symptoms before?	What could I have done better?

Takeaways:

THE ORANGE RHINO CHALLENGE TRIGGER TRACKING SHEET

Day and time	Whom I yelled at	Supposed Trigger	How I felt at the time? Anything bothering me?	What was I doing before I felt the urge to yell?	What were kids doing, if applicable?	Were kids hungry, thirsty, tired?	Did I feel any physical symptoms before?	What could I have done better?

Takeaways:

Acknowledgments

This book would not exist if it were not for the incredible, mind-blowing support and love I received from so many people. Every time I wanted to quit The Orange Rhino Challenge or stop writing because I felt overwhelmed and doubted my abilities, each and every one of these people, perhaps knowingly, more likely unknowingly, found a way to help me believe in myself and to keep moving forward toward my goal. For that I am forever, forever grateful. (Shoot, more tears on the computer again!)

First and foremost, I would like to thank my husband for believing in me before I truly believed in myself! I thank you, dear, for constantly—I mean constantly—listening to me when I felt down and encouraging me to keep going. For the first time in a long while I don't feel like a quitter and that's because you wouldn't let me quit.

To my boys, James, Edward, Andrew, and Mac, for giving me a reason to push myself every day to be the best that I can be. Yes, thank you for your shenanigans, for while frustrating in the moment, they ultimately helped me grow as a mom and a person. I am in a much better place today because of you. Thank you for being the best Orange Rhino supporters ever!

To my parents, thank you for always believing in me and supporting my dreams. A special thanks for your babysitting support during the writing of this book; I know you sacrificed a lot of personal time and I am most appreciative!

To my friends, thank you for constantly asking about my journey, lending a listening ear when I needed to yell, and dropping off Orange Rhino–themed gifts when I needed to be inspired. You all brought countless smiles to my face and I feel beyond blessed to call you my friends. Many thanks also to all the therapists and teachers in my boys' lives who not only gave me invaluable tips on how to better cope with my particular parenting challenges, but also gave me (and my boys) much love and support.

To Brooke Linville at Digavise, thank you for taking my vision for my blog and bringing it to life. But more than that, thank you for your friendship, your guidance, and your constant encouragement. You were a pillar of strength and knowledge for me during my journey. Many thanks also to Christine DeSavino for taking my vision for the photographs in this book and not just delivering, but overdelivering!

To The Orange Rhino Challenge community, thank you for believing in me, encouraging me, and inspiring me daily with your own stories of efforts to yell less and love more. Our community is a rare place of love, support, and nonjudgment and has been the greatest gift to me, and all of us. Thank you for making it exist and for helping it grow. Every post you shared, and every comment you made, helped us reach more and more parents—and by default, kids—with our message. Collectively, we, especially you, opened up the conversation about yelling and helped so many. Know that I yell less and love more because of you, and that not only I, but also and perhaps more importantly, my four boys, thank you!

To Gail O'Connor at *Parents* magazine, thank you for urging me to consider writing a book, for seeing possibilities in me that I didn't see, and for sharing my blog with your audience, thus helping me increase readership and ultimately help more parents feel less guilty at night about their yelling. I also thank those at Huffington Post Parents for sharing my "10 Things I Learned When I Stopped Yelling at My Kids" article, for that, too, greatly increased my ability to reach more parents.

To Rachel Macy Stafford of Hands Free Mama, Shawn Fink of Awesomely Awake, and all the other bloggers I met on my journey: Thank you for being a sounding board when I got lost in the blogging and parenting world; thank you for supporting my message and sharing it so readily; and thank you for being you—phenomenally inspiring people, friends, and parents.

And last but most certainly not the least, to Amanda Waddell at Fairwinds Press, thank you for finding me when I needed to be found. Thank you to everyone else who touched this book. I have dreamed of writing a book since I was in high school and you have made that dream a reality, especially Winnie Prentiss, Betsy Gammons, Katie Fawkes, and Anne Re. Thank you for understanding and embracing me and my message and for helping me reach even more people than I ever imagined.

About the Author

Sheila McCraith, also known as The Orange Rhino, is a mom to four energetic boys now ages eight and under. In January 2012 her handyman caught her screaming at her boys, giving her the final encouragement needed to find a way to kick her yelling habit to the curb. The Orange Rhino Challenge, her public promise to go 365 days straight without yelling and her commitment to no longer parent like a gray rhino, a naturally peaceful animal who charges and becomes aggressive when provoked, but to parent instead with warmth, patience, and the determination to remain calm, was born shortly after that mortifying-turned-inspiring day. She successfully achieved her goal by a wide margin, crediting much of that success to finding a fun and creative way to tackle a not-so-fun problem and the incredible Orange Rhino community. She continues to be an Orange Rhino to this day.

To hold herself accountable during her challenge, and to find support she knew she desperately needed, she decided to keep a public blog, www.TheOrangeRhino.com. Her blog documents her journey, highlighting her lessons learned and top alternatives to yelling. Written in an honest, approachable, sometimes humorous, and oftentimes inspiring voice, the blog has created a comfortable forum for parents and others to openly discuss their mutual desire to stop yelling and to find the support so many crave. Sheila's blog won *Parents* magazine's 2013 Blog Most Likely to Help You Achieve a Goal and has been featured numerous times on the Huffington Post and other top parenting and educational blogs around the world.

Before staying at home, Sheila worked in brand marketing and used to constantly debate starting her own company around one of her many passions: cake decorating, photography, or doing random acts of kindness. The Orange Rhino blog and community helped her discover, though, that sharing her struggles and triumphs in order to help others is exactly how she wants to spend her free time.